Left for Dead

Left for Dead

A Second Life after Vietnam

Jon Hovde and
Maureen Anderson

University of Minnesota Press
Minneapolis • London

MINNESOTA

The lines from an untitled poem by Robert Godbout in chapter 8 are reprinted
by permission of the author.

Published by the University of Minnesota Press
111 Third Avenue South, Suite 290
Minneapolis, MN 55401-2520
http://www.upress.umn.edu

Library of Congress Cataloging-in-Publication Data

Hovde, Jon.
    Left for dead : a second life after Vietnam / Jon Hovde and Maureen Anderson.
        p. cm.
    ISBN 0-8166-4624-4 (alk. paper)
    1. Hovde, Jon. 2. Vietnamese Conflict, 1961–1975—Veterans—United States—Biography.
3. Vietnamese Conflict, 1961–1975—Personal narratives, American. 4. Disabled veterans—
United States—Biography. I. Anderson, Maureen. II. Title.
    DS559.73.U6H68 2005
    959.704'342'092—dc22

2004023013

Printed in the United States of America on acid-free paper

The University of Minnesota is an equal-opportunity educator and employer.

12 11 10 09 08 07 06 05   10 9 8 7 6 5 4 3 2 1

To the memory of Chaplain Donald Ostroot and Father J. E. Vessels

To the memory of my father, Ole Hovde,
and to Darlene
—J.H.

To Darrell and Katie
and to my parents
—M.A.

Contents

Preface

Once was enough.

After you make it through a tour of duty in Vietnam, the last thing you want to do is watch movies about it. Not that I haven't seen a few. *Platoon* wasn't bad—in terms of what it was like to battle mosquitoes if not the enemy. But I couldn't make it through *We Were Soldiers*. I just couldn't handle it.

A lot of veterans feel the same way, from what they tell me.

One of them is Len McLean. He finally got around to seeing *Forrest Gump* in 1998. He rented the video and watched it with his daughter. He was doing okay, he said, until he got to the part where Gary Sinise, as the wounded Lieutenant Dan Taylor, lights into Gump—who had saved his life.

Now, you listen to me. We all have a destiny. Nothin' just happens. It's all part of a plan. I should have died out there with my men. But now I'm nothin' but a goddamn cripple, a legless freak. Look. Look. Look at me! Do you see that? Do you know what it's like not to be able to use your legs?

Did you hear what I said? You cheated me! I had a destiny. I was supposed to die in the field with honor. That was my destiny and you cheated me out of it. Do you understand what I'm saying, Gump? This wasn't supposed to happen. Not to me. I had a destiny.

Look at me! What am I gonna do now?

What am I gonna do now?

McLean had never talked about the war, not really, not in any great detail. But now suddenly, there he was, telling his daughter about the Minnesota boy he had rescued—only to have him die at the 12th Evac Hospital in Cu Chi. The nineteen-year-old had lost an arm and a leg when the armored personnel carrier (APC) he was driving had hit an antitank mine. The force of the explosion had blown the engine half a football field away.

"I wonder how he would feel if he had lived," McLean said. "Would he thank me or hate me?"

"I think you're about to find out," his daughter told him the very next morning.

Because there I was, on the front page of the *Albuquerque Journal*. The paper had done a big story on my reunion with my nurse, Kay Layman, who lives thirty minutes from McLean.

I had no idea the two were neighbors.

McLean had no idea I hadn't been dead for thirty years.

His daughter called first, and my wife took the message. "My dad is the medic who got Jon from the helicopter to the hospital," she said. "Do you think he'd like to talk to him?"

Would I.

"How could you possibly have remembered me after all these years?" I wanted to know.

"First of all," McLean said, "your name is unusual. Second, you were the worst case I saw in Vietnam who didn't die instantly. When I dropped you off at the evac, they told me you wouldn't make it. I never considered the possibility you would."

Now it was his turn. "Jon," he said, "I have to ask." There

was a pause while he tried to compose himself. "Are you glad I saved you, or do you hate me for it?"

"You're kidding," I said. "Do you really think I could hate you for saving my life?" That would be like hating my mother for bringing me into the world. It would never occur to me.

But how would he know? A lot had happened since they sent my squad leader back to the APC to retrieve my leg—not to reattach it, just to make sure as much of me as possible made it home for burial.

It's like I told him, there's so much more to my life than a war story. But that is where it all begins.

Acknowledgments

I wanted to write this book. I tried for years, but couldn't do it. Without an army of friends and family, I might have given up. And without Maureen, it might have never happened.

Thanks first to Darlene, for her love, compassion, and understanding—always. To my children and grandchildren, for whom I started writing to begin with: Jeremy, Sarah, and Preston Jon . . . and Jessica, Nate, and Olivia Dawn.

To my mother, Arleene, with all my love. I'm glad you can see our story here. To my sisters, Barb, Karen, Cathy, and Lana. You gave me more reasons to find my way home. Thanks to my extended family: the people of Fertile, and the members of Concordia Lutheran.

To my good friends Clark Dyrud and Roger Bengtson, for everything.

To the thousands of kids across the country who have listened to me speak. I cherish each of your letters.

To Kay Layman, Len McLean, Bruce Ashworth, and Randy Scott, for keeping me alive in Vietnam. To Drs. Bruce Ring and Dave Peterson, who are still keeping me alive and walking.

Special thanks to the families of Richard Godbout and

Leslie Cowden. Both men were my friends. Les saved my life. The people who love them were very gracious to help with this book, and it is also dedicated to them.

—Jon Hovde

I did not want to write this book. You can ask Roxann Daggett. Her son is married to Jon Hovde's niece, and she thought Jon had a great story. I was sure he did, but I wasn't interested.

The minute I said no, I felt guilty. I've always ached for people who have gone off to war—including my dad, who served in Korea—and this would be a way to show that appreciation. So thanks to Roxann, for telling Jon about me. And to Adrienne Buboltz, for the same.

It wasn't just the guilt that got to me. It was the chance to work with Todd Orjala and the rest of my friends at the University of Minnesota Press. Thanks to each of you, for your attention to every detail. There will be more cookies in your Christmas stocking.

Thanks to Rick Shefchik at the *St. Paul Pioneer Press*, for the first pass. To Jon's friends, who helped polish the manuscript— Clark Dyrud, Kay Layman, Ned Seachrist, and Randy Scott. Clark and Kay especially: I owe you. To Jon's family, who probably missed him while we worked on this book. You can have him back now.

My heartfelt thanks to Jamie Marks Erickson, for the editing and the empathy. To Ellen Kensinger and Cindy Wear, for more of the same. To Beth Walter, who got lunch postponed— for a year. And Margaret Hart, who helped me change careers and made sure I never looked back.

Special thanks to a veteran of the Gulf War, Dr. Thomas Seaworth, for sharing his expertise on medical and military matters.

To Katie Anderson, my fountain of inspiration. Thanks for letting me see the world through your eyes and showing me what I have missed.

A dozen long-stemmed roses to Darrell Anderson, who spent more time researching this book and editing it than I did writing it. Everything worthwhile begins with you. Thanks for signing up, holding on, and never laughing just to be polite.

Finally, thanks to Jon, for not taking no for an answer.

—Maureen Anderson

Maureen and Jon are eager to hear how this book touched you, and Jon is available for public appearances and speaking engagements. You are encouraged to contact them through e-mail at feedback@leftfordeadthebook.com or visit their Web site at www.leftfordeadthebook.com.

CHAPTER 1

Death Rolls In

"We are now entering Vietnam air space."

That's what we were told after twenty hours in the air on the seventh of October, 1967. Twenty hours of feeling like someone was holding hot irons to my chest, twenty hours of feeling crushed under the weight of my dread. Before the pilot's words had registered, and I'm talking seconds, there was a fighter jet off each wing of our TWA airplane. I think they were F-4s, but whatever they were, I swear they were close enough to touch.

And I thought to myself, how bad is it where we're going that we need a fighter jet off each wing? I felt like the cartoon character who barrels off a cliff and doesn't start falling until he realizes his predicament.

Which is what happened next. The pilot came back on and said this wasn't going to be a normal landing, so be prepared: "We're going to descend very quickly." No kidding. Before I had time to brace myself, boom, just like that, my heart was in my throat and we were on the ground. To this day I cannot believe a TWA jet can drop that fast and land safely. But we did.

You have to land quickly, of course, to keep the Vietcong from taking out 150 men at once. I tried to look at it philosophically: the faster we land, the faster I'll be a few seconds closer to getting the hell out of here.

The door to the plane opened and in it came—death. I swear to God you could smell death from that very moment. It just rolled in like a fog until you thought you would choke on the stench. I started to shiver. "God, what *is* this place?" I wondered.

Then, just like that, I got promoted. This guy jumped on the plane, wearing a flak jacket and a steel helmet—which we called a pot—and carrying an M-16 rifle. He was at the front of the cabin when he hollered, "Welcome to Vietnam. President Johnson has just ordered that no one less than a PFC will be killed in Vietnam." Most of us were E-2s. A PFC is one grade higher, E-3. "So any of you who are E-2s," he continued, "you just got promoted to E-3." Pause. "In case you're killed getting off the plane."

Yeah, right. That's what I thought. Granted the air was thick with death, but I just couldn't believe we'd be killed right away. Maybe when you're nineteen you don't believe you'll die. Even in war, death was always something that happened to the other guy. A couple of buddies from my hometown of Fertile, Minnesota, took out insurance policies for losing limbs, or worse, in Vietnam. It was really cheap, but I didn't want any part of it. I didn't want to do anything that would make me think about dying.

We had landed at the army base in Bien Hoa. That's where all the planes took off from. Whether you were coming or going, Bien Hoa was it. In fact there was a planeload of guys waiting to board when we got off. Their 365 days were up and they were going home. Short-timers, they were called, and I wished I could trade places with them. Oh, I wished. "Short! Short! Short!" they were hollering. They were dressed in fatigues just like us, and they didn't appear that different. You might think they'd look emaciated or haggard, but they didn't, not really. They were just happy. Drinking, smoking, partying, whatever. They didn't seem like they felt particularly sorry for us, either. They probably thought, hey, we've done our time and now it's someone else's turn. I know I would have.

I found out later that guys had been killed boarding their plane home. This was Vietnam. You weren't safe anywhere.

So they loaded us into snub-nosed buses, green and brown camouflage, but more brown than green, for the trip to the 90th Replacement Center. There were probably fifty of us in each one. Once we pulled out of the air base we started to see more of the country. Just rice fields, really. And . . . green. It was green and lush as any pictures you've seen. We passed through several small villages and saw people in black pajamas and black cone hats. I wondered if they were the enemy. What struck me most was the heavy wire covering all the windows of the bus. It almost looked like chicken wire, but you could tell it was a lot heavier. I found out later it was to keep the VC from tossing grenades through a window and blowing up everyone inside.

I should have been terrified, but I felt a strange sense of relief. My tour had started, and it was time to see things for myself, do my job, and get home. For months I had lived and breathed war from a distance. Now I was finally going to experience it for myself, and I wanted to get it over with.

It was maybe ten miles to the 90th Replacement Center. We grabbed our duffel bags, got off the bus, and settled into our barracks. It was like any other base camp: a lot of tin buildings with cement floors, long narrow buildings with cots in them. And for a couple of days we just hung out. We sat around and talked, wrote letters, played cards, that sort of thing. It got old fast. I was sick of hanging out. We'd already hung out at the air bases in Oakland and Travis. That was the army, though—hurry up and wait.

I took for granted that John Collins and I would get assigned to the same outfit. He was in jungle training with me in

Fort Gordon, Georgia, and had been with me on the plane out here. But when we got our orders, he was the last assigned to the 1st Infantry Division. I was called next. I was going with the 25th Infantry Division, Company A 4th of the 23rd. My outfit was called the Tomahawks and was based in Cu Chi, about twenty-five miles northwest of Saigon.

I was crushed. I'd already said enough goodbyes for one lifetime before I got on the plane.

I was taken to the base camp in Cu Chi by helicopter. I'd never been on one before and it was exciting. You're sitting outside, basically, and what struck me was how low we flew. We just skimmed the tops of the trees. I would later learn that the VC got a hundred dollars, American, if they took a helicopter down. It didn't matter how many were on board, which in our case would have been just two pilots and me. Supposedly the average annual income for a Vietnamese family was less than three hundred dollars, so that was a lot of money.

It was on that flight that I let myself think about how alone I was. Twelve thousand miles from home might as well have been from here to the moon. Three hundred and sixty-five days might as well have been life without parole—that's how long it seemed I'd be over there. I was already sick I was so lonesome. And now, no John.

It's not that I suddenly started having regrets. That wasn't it. In thirty-seven years I've never felt a twinge of regret for signing up. I didn't volunteer for the army. If you did, you were considered RA, regular army, and that meant a three-year hitch. I found out that you could volunteer for the draft, and if you did you got a two-year hitch, one of which would almost certainly be in Vietnam. I volunteered for the draft. That also gave me forty-five days or so before I had to report for duty. Had I waited to be drafted, I might have had only a week or two.

It didn't occur to me to move to Canada or change religions or even go to college, not for one moment. Though for a while I didn't think I'd have to serve after all. I'd been working as a journeyman carpenter for my uncle in California, and one day I busted the heel of my left foot when I fell off a roof. The doctor told me I wouldn't be able to walk on rough ground after that. "So much for Vietnam," I thought—until the day of my physical. The guy ahead of me had a really bad back, but not so bad he couldn't be a combat soldier, or so they told him. "I suppose my heel won't matter," I told the doctor. You got that right, I think he said.

It wasn't the letdown you might imagine. I was that devoted to my country. As an only son I wouldn't have had to sign up. My parents wanted to pull the approved strings, but I said if they did I wouldn't come home anyway.

A lot of guys in my high school class got deferments for college, and some still feel so guilty they're living the same hell they were trying to escape. I was committed to my country, it was my turn, it was that simple. You might think, well, he was nineteen and naive. But those feelings of what I call patriotism hold up decades later.

The helicopter landed in Cu Chi, Vietnam, and a guy picked me up in a jeep. He worked in the office at Company A 4/23 Mechanized, where I was going to be stationed. He took me into the base camp and I signed the usual mountain of paperwork. One of the first things you found out was the date you could leave. In my case that was October 7, 1968.

I hung out for a few more days at base camp, where I would be attending classes for a week. Orientation to Vietnam. All the things you never wanted to know that your life now depended on. I still felt lonesome, but you bond pretty quickly and I was getting to know some of the guys. Food at the base bordered on real food, and except for filling sandbags and whatever other detail you pulled, it wasn't the worst. There was plenty of time to write letters and hang out. Too much time, actually. More hurry up and wait.

I soon cursed myself for cursing the boredom.

One day early on I ran into a classmate from Fertile. Yeah, Fertile, population 900. What do you think the odds were that we'd run into each other half a world away? I saw Keith Bolstad at the base exchange, and we agreed to meet up that evening. It was always very dark at night. I was used to pitch-black nights in rural Minnesota, but they were nothing like this. It was disorienting. I was walking the dirt road to Keith's outfit when the sky exploded. "Mortar attack!" guys hollered. "Oh God," I thought. "What do I do?" I started running and dove into the nearest sandbag bunker. I heard more explosions and then the alarms. They almost sounded like tornado sirens. They blared and blared while I tried to figure out what the hell was happening. I huddled with some guys until the explosions stopped.

We never saw the enemy, and I don't think anyone was hurt that night. But decades later, I still find it difficult to get to sleep.

The classroom version of Vietnam orientation began a few days afterward, from nine in the morning until four in the afternoon. We sat on bleachers and listened to guys talking about what we'd likely encounter when we got to the field. Our base camp was positioned over a VC tunnel complex. I don't think anyone at the time even knew how massive that tunnel system was. I didn't until many years later, when I read *The Tunnels of Cu Chi*. The VC were jungle fighters. That's all some of them did their entire lives, from back when they were fighting the French. They'd jump out of the tunnels, shoot at you and draw fire back, then get back down and run. There wasn't a lot of hand-to-hand. Before they attacked, they'd smoke marijuana for courage. You'd smell that and you knew—you knew you were in for it. To this day I can pick up a marijuana smell from miles away.

You might think our soldiers were doing the same thing, and some of them were. I knew guys who traded cartons of cigarettes for shoeboxes full of pot from the Vietnamese who were friendly to us. Almost everyone smoked cigarettes, including me, and there was a lot of drinking. I probably didn't drink six beers the entire time I was in Vietnam, although I made up for that afterward. But for the most part we were cleaner than you might imagine. My language was as colorful as the next guy's, but not in my letters home. I said "dang" a lot in those letters, believe it or not— "Dang this, dang that." My girlfriend, Darlene, who's now my wife, saved every letter I wrote to her from Vietnam and everything's "dang." People read them now and think I had to be smoking something to talk like that. But that was just me, a small-town boy from Minnesota.

It was in orientation that we learned about punji pits, one of so many ways the VC tried to kill us. A punji pit was just a square hole in the ground with bamboo canes sticking up from the bottom, but it was covered with leaves and whatever else so you wouldn't know it was there. The canes were sharp, and if you fell on one it would punch you right through the foot. Not only that, but the VC would urinate and defecate on them so your wounds would get infected. Often it wasn't the wound that killed you, but the infection. Again, I didn't know about some of this until after I got home. It made me wonder if I was better off not knowing when I was there. It wasn't even so much that people in charge were holding back. The war was just really gearing up when I arrived in 1967. My base camp had been established just the year before. I'm sure there were some things even the instructors didn't know.

There were a lot of different ways the VC got you, of course.

They'd run a thin wire between trees and tie a hand grenade to it, so if you tripped that wire it pulled the pin and the grenade blew up.

Every kind of booby trap we were likely to encounter they wanted us to see in class first. I saw a punji pit and the wire, and I can still see them. You never forget.

The thing that stands out most about orientation was when they told us what might happen if we were taken prisoner. I'd already heard plenty about the torture, and couldn't imagine becoming a POW and surviving. They told us the VC put you in little cages. They'd have one bullet and five blanks in their gun and play all kinds of games with you. They'd stake you to the ground with no clothes on and let the mosquitoes eat you alive. Everything you've ever heard, and worse, that's what they were telling us to expect. Years in a little cage, being tortured any number of ways and eventually killed anyway.

The instructor told us, "The one thing you don't have to worry about in the Cu Chi district is being taken POW." Before it could even register what great news that was, he continued. "Because they'll kill you."

You might think my heart would have sunk hearing that, but it didn't. To me it was a relief that at least I wouldn't be a POW. The relief didn't last long, because he wasn't finished: "But how you die is not very pleasant. So we need you to remember this: if you do get captured, make sure you've saved a bullet for yourself. Kill yourself before they get to you because if they do, they will literally skin you alive. You will die a horrible, slow death. Don't let that happen." He paused. "Every one of them could probably kill you in a different way."

Most of the VC were Buddhists, or so we were told. They supposedly believed that when they killed an American soldier, if they cut the ears, the nose, and the genitals off, he wouldn't come back as a male. He wouldn't come back to fight.

In orientation they walked that fine line between preparing you for battle and encouraging you to kill yourself right there to spare yourself the horror of what lay ahead. It dawned on me immediately—no wonder they only drafted young people. Teenagers drive like maniacs and take all kinds of chances because they don't believe they'll die. I was listening to all this training as if what they talked about would only happen to someone else.

In theory I knew what I'd do if I was about to be killed. If I got within a block of a VC, I'd turn the gun on myself. I was absolutely prepared to do that, and absolutely sure I wouldn't need to.

To the extent there was any comfort in what I was learning, it was that everyone in my outfit said we would never leave a man behind. Dead or alive, he would not be left behind. We would all perish before we'd let that happen, and I really believed that. It felt good to know I would not be left out there by myself to be butchered.

One day in training they had a dog up front, a very normal-looking German shepherd. "Most leg outfits will have a dog like this," the instructor told us. Mine wasn't going to—we had all the big guns—but we still had to know about the dogs. "The dog is trained to one man. Listen very closely now. You don't do anything with this dog. Don't walk up to pet it, don't talk to it, don't do anything. This dog is trained to kill and he will kill you. He'll jump up, get you right here by the jugular, pull like this, and kill you instantly."

The dogs were trained to one man for one year. At the end of the year the soldier went home, but the dog was killed. It was too expensive to retrain it to another man, and you just wouldn't do it. And for all the denial I'd been in about the possibility of my own death, I took the death of these dogs hard. It didn't seem fair. We got to go home to our families but the dog gets the dart. It just seemed cruel. That bothered Keith, too, when he heard about it.

On the other hand, he was as amused as I was to hear that one day out in the field my squad leader took a .50 caliber to this huge bird sitting on top of a tree. It was probably a quarter mile away, and after Clark had at it all you could see were a few feathers floating down. He just blew the shit out of that poor bird.

We never thought about what day it was in Vietnam. All we knew was how many days we had left: 292 days left, 288 days left. Every time I wrote home it was always how many days left. I thought we'd get all new camouflage clothes when we arrived, but instead I wore the same greens I had worn in boot camp. When it started to get warm I took my shirt off and left my flak jacket open. The flak jacket was just a heavy vest and we were supposed to wear it all the time. It weighed four or five pounds and protected us from shrapnel. Then we had the pot, our helmet, that we were also supposed to wear all the time. It was solid steel, with a strap, and it also weighed about four pounds. I didn't wear it much. It was too damn hot and heavy. I wore a jungle hat instead.

The heat was oppressive. It was usually at least ninety-five, from what I remember. And the rain! When I got there it was still monsoon season and it rained twenty-four hours a day. In Minnesota the rain would have meant a break from mosquitoes, but not here. Back home they joked about the mosquito being the state bird, but they're gnats compared to the Vietnam variety. You remember that scene in *Platoon* where Charlie Sheen's character is trying to bat away mosquitoes (the bites are welts, and he's covered in them) in an endless downpour? That was Vietnam. You want to know what it's like? That's what it was like. You're covered in welts, you're sore, you itch so bad you think you'll go crazy just from that, and there's no relief. It's not like you can use spray because the VC would sniff you out even faster.

Here's how dumb I was. I thought, well, I don't know how

many showers I'll be taking in Vietnam so I'd better pack some cologne. The first time I broke that out I almost got tackled. "You stupid shit," I think someone said. They were laughing, but they were serious. "Bury that damn bottle." Somewhere in Vietnam there's a bottle of Jade East deep beneath the ground. I buried that sucker right there, right on the spot.

The mosquitoes weren't quite so bad in base camp. We slept in bunkers and had netting to give us a little protection. We felt a little safer from the mosquitoes, and we felt a little safer from the enemy. Sure, once night came we were under fire a lot of the time, but it almost seemed like the VC were trying to harass us as much as kill us. They wanted to make sure we never slept soundly, and we never did.

On about my third day of orientation I was issued my M-16 rifle. It was almost like a driver's license. You weren't really a soldier until you had your M-16.

Then there was the requisite KP duty, kitchen police. We'd work in the mess hall, helping the cooks peel potatoes or whatever. One of the most coveted jobs was shit burner. The latrines were like the outhouses you may remember from the old days, but in this case it was just the top cut off of a 55-gallon drum—which was slid under a hole. When the crap started building up the shit burner came out with a can of diesel fuel and burned it all up. Then he slid the clean can back under the hole. When everyone was back at base camp he was a busy guy, but he had a relatively nice life. He got to sit back at camp, where the mosquitoes weren't so bad, he got hot meals every day, and he had a cot to sleep on.

Heaven.

I was not so lucky. After orientation I was sent out into the field. My outfit was working in the Ho Bo Woods, part of the Iron Triangle. The Iron Triangle was a VC stronghold near Cu Chi, situated between two converging rivers. We were in what was called the Filhol Rubber Plantation. Michelin rubber, that is, where the tires come from. We were knocking down rubber trees so the VC wouldn't have them to hide in and move through. It was called Operation Barking Sands.

It was late afternoon when I got to my track, track 23. That's what we called APCs, armored personnel carriers. They looked like small tanks. The guys were just standing around when I arrived. The first person I saw was wearing a flak jacket with a map of Minnesota on it, and there was a star on it near where Fertile is. I couldn't believe it. Oh God, I thought, he's from northern Minnesota. What are the odds of this, I wondered, twelve thousand miles from home? We introduced ourselves. Turns out he was my squad leader, Clark Dyrud from Thief River Falls. I was stunned. Thief River's about fifty miles from Fertile. Clark was the nicest guy, and I liked him instantly. Maybe things were going to be okay after all.

I settled into life in Vietnam, if you can call it that. The first night I slept on top of the APC because all the benches inside the track were taken. The radio was going off all the time, though, and between that and my mattress of steel I didn't sleep much. I was so dog-ass tired by the next night I thought I had to find a way to get some rest. I blew up my air mattress and cursed myself for not thinking of that the night before, but the guys were laughing at me again. I woke up at one point in the pouring rain—it was always pouring rain—and I didn't recognize anyone around me. I'd floated away from my unit. Not only that, but the air mattress had a hole in it, so that was the end of that. No wonder the guys were laughing.

We got up about five in the morning. If we weren't in what they called a hot zone, breakfast was flown in by helicopter. We were served eggs out of a garbage can, believe it or not, which tasted like crap. You could get toast, too, and coffee or iced tea. I had toast with coffee or tea, but never the eggs—I never got hungry enough for them to sound good.

I always woke up stiff and sore, wishing I were home if only to take a shower. There were showers at base camp like you might have seen in the TV show *M*A*S*H*, but at the track you just stunk. It bothered some guys more than others. They'd take off all their clothes and we took turns pouring water from our pots over them. That's what I used to shave in the morning, water in my steel pot. It helped me feel a little bit clean.

The biggest hygiene problem was your feet. Many of us left our boots on all the time. You wouldn't want to get hit by the VC at night and have to go find your boots and put them on before you could return fire. So a lot of guys got jungle rot. It was a constant battle.

My outfit was responsible for clearing the jungle. We pulled security for the Rome plows, which pushed down rubber trees. They were called Rome plows because they were made in Rome, Georgia. They looked like bulldozers. We were just tearing up ground, basically, fifteen thousand acres or so of land that had to be cleared. But it wasn't like we got to avoid conflict that way. It wasn't the front lines and the back lines in Vietnam. It was just . . . Vietnam. Wherever you were, it was combat.

There were usually five Rome plows going around in a circle, pushing the trees down. I was on one of several tracks going around them, trying to keep them safe.

We pulled out every morning at seven. I sat on top of the track with my M-16 rifle, loaded, the safety on. Most guys had the safety off unless they were putting the rifle down or something. The gun had a little lever that you clicked for semiautomatic or fully automatic. On fully automatic it was like a machine gun. You could empty a clip of nineteen rounds in about three seconds—

nothing you'd want to do accidentally, and I was a little skittish about it.

We always left one or two guys back where we were positioned the night before, just to protect the perimeter. The perimeter was a circle, maybe a hundred yards in diameter, where the tracks parked at night. The Rome plows dug out parts of the perimeter to help hide the tracks and tanks. It was almost like a wagon train, except the tops of the vehicles were level with the ground. The Rome plows and other equipment were then parked inside that circle.

When we first got to the area we were going to clear that day we lined up everything we had—tracks, tanks, whatever—and had what we called a cookoff. We shot rounds like crazy into the brush, 105s, .50 calibers, everything. This was just to make sure our weapons functioned. The humidity caused a lot of problems. A bonus was that you might kill any enemy who was hiding there. If there were some unexploded bombs you wanted to pick those off too, get rid of the mines if you could, and so on. The cookoffs probably didn't last five minutes. We just blasted away. We didn't wear earplugs either. You might wonder how any of us have any hearing left, but actually there are only two tones I miss in a hearing test these days. Go figure.

Once we were done with the cookoff, we took our positions on the APC and made our first cut through the woods. On a good day we'd clear thirteen acres. We just knocked the trees down as opposed to cleaning them out or anything. The goal was simply to clear the area so the VC could be spotted from our aircraft during the day.

My job was just to sit on top of the track and look for VC. I was scared, especially at first, especially considering what I'd heard about how you never saw the enemy. The jungle was very dense, and that first pass was treacherous. We were looking for the black pajama gang, as we called them, VC that couldn't have been eighty-five pounds soaking wet. When days went by and we didn't see them, we started to relax a little. But we shouldn't have.

We ate C rations in the field. The C stands for combat. They came in a little brown box, maybe ten or twelve to a case. The squad leader usually got the first pick, then the driver, all the way down to the new guy. Each one had a different meal. The most god-awful stuff was ham and lima beans. Everything was in a can. Probably 90 percent of the time I took the chicken noodle soup. It also had crackers with peanut butter. I love peanut butter and that was the only C that had peanut butter in it. There was also pound cake in a can, a pack of four cigarettes (believe it or not), and some kind of powdered chocolate bar that tasted like shit. It was horrible. I used to save them because when we went through the villages I could throw them to the kids who were starving. You'd have to be pretty hungry to eat that crap. We just drank warm water unless someone on the track had pop.

Meal preparation was a little primitive. All you had was a can opener and some explosive. The can openers we called P-38s, just little wire things you kept on a keychain. The explosive was C-4. It almost looked like a two-pound brick of cheese. We'd tear off a little piece of that, set it on top of the track and light it. Then we'd hold our cans over that with pliers or something and they'd be hot in seconds. When everyone was finished, you'd just let it burn out. You might think I was green, but there were guys who were worse off. One day a rookie who wasn't familiar with C-4 and was the last to heat his food stomped on it afterward to put the fire out. He blew his foot off right there.

At five o'clock we'd head back to the perimeter. By then you're hot, you're more sunburned than the day before—I was sent back to base camp at one point early on because I was blistered up that bad—and you're exhausted. The day's work was far from over, though. We never stayed in an area more than three nights, so we were always either getting set up or preparing to move again. Supplies were flown in at night, and there was always sandbagging and other chores to do until dark.

There was a break between that and bedtime, when guys played cards, wrote letters, and listened to Armed Forces Radio. Talk about pleasure! You listened to the same songs your girlfriend was listening to, and looked up at the same moon she was looking at. And for a few minutes you forgot about the mortar fire and the mosquitoes and the jungle rot. Clark was hung up on the song, "Ode to Billie Joe." He could be in the middle of a poop meeting—where he got our assignment for the next day—and that song would come on and he'd say, "Hold it, I want to hear this." The reception on those little transistor radios we had in the field was terrible. Clark wanted to figure out what was being thrown off the Tallahatchie Bridge.

Night was the worst. We prayed for daylight because the bugs were so bad. The only protection in the field was what we called a shelter half, just a piece of plastic that we kind of pinned up to keep the worst of the rain and bugs off of us. We didn't need much in the way of a blanket because it only got down to the sixties at night.

There was no such thing as REM sleep. We had to take turns, every night, sitting behind a .50-caliber machine gun and staying in radio contact with our company commander. We called it the TC hatch—I think it stood for track commander's hatch—and we rotated that duty all night. That's why we liked to be at full-strength, nine or so men to a track. That wasn't the way it worked, of course. Most of the time we had only seven and often there were only five. If you were the track driver you'd get the first and last shifts in the TC hatch and get the most uninterrupted sleep because you were driving during the day and had to be alert.

But each of us pulled two shifts a night, for forty-five minutes or so depending on how many guys there were. If you were lucky enough to get to sleep at all, next thing you knew you'd be awakened and assume your position in the hatch. "Sit rep negative," you'd say into the radio. Situation report negative. Nothing happening. You hoped.

We weren't supposed to smoke when we were behind the .50 caliber because the VC could spot the red glow of the cigarette for miles, or so we were told. Most of us did, though. How would you stay awake otherwise? A lot of guys cupped it in their hands. Me, I got to a point where once I got a cigarette about halfway down I could roll it inside my mouth. The company commander always warned us he might check up on us to make sure we were alert. "And I don't ever want to see anybody smoking cigarettes," he'd add, but I knew I had a way around it. To this day people can't figure out how I could smoke a cigarette inside my mouth without it burning my tongue, but I could. I'd keep it in there, lit, and not have the CO know I was smoking. I've done it hundreds of times and never burned my tongue. If I failed as a soldier, I thought, I could always join the circus.

Manning the TC hatch was like being a lifeguard on *Baywatch* compared to the other assignments we rotated at night. There were two: listening post and ambush patrol. My first night on ambush patrol one of the guys just about hurt himself he was laughing so hard at me. It was because you could take as much ammunition as you wanted, and my flak jacket was weighed down with it. I had stuffed all my pockets with hand grenades. It was only my third night in the field, and I wasn't taking any chances. I had so many grenades and so many clips for my M-16 this guy told me I could hold off a whole battalion of VC by myself.

Ambush patrol was basically just pulling security for the perimeter. The perimeter was probably three or four miles from where we were pushing down trees (though it varied) and guys on ambush patrol were probably a mile or so outside the perimeter. We talked in terms of clicks: one click was a kilometer. There were eight or nine of us who went out, one guy from each track. One was the radio man. His job wasn't so much to fight the war as it was to make sure we stayed in communication with the old man—that's what we called our CO, the commanding officer.

The listening post was like ambush patrol, except fewer guys, maybe just three. That duty felt safer because you were a lot closer to the perimeter. You could literally run back and dive into a bunker if you drew fire. The ambush patrol was hung out there by itself. You had radio contact and that was about it.

Before we went on ambush we put on camouflage paint. It came in tubes of green, brown, tan, and black cream. On my first night on ambush, we were already out of camouflage, so I just picked up a handful of dirt and rubbed my face with it. It felt like I was using sandpaper. When we came back to the perimeter the next morning I washed my face with water from my steel pot. Later, when we got more tubes of camouflage cream, I found I actually liked using dirt more because it didn't seal up your pores and your skin could breathe. Of course the black guys didn't have this problem.

On ambush we just walked out to where we were supposed to be, carrying our M-16s. This was one time I wore my steel pot, my flak jacket, anything and everything that would help me feel a little safer. When we got to our spot we literally just lay down on the ground. The eight or ten of us were all in a row. Then we took turns staying awake. We'd start at one end and pull shifts of thirty minutes, again depending on how many guys we had. My first night on ambush I was about in the middle of the pack. We were lying there on this dirt road, it was darker than hell, and we couldn't see anything. I was so scared. All our big guns were more than a mile away and I felt very vulnerable. Though right away I couldn't imagine anything the VC could do to us that would be worse than the mosquitoes. All night long we fed the damn things, and there was no relief. I prayed for daylight. Please God, let the sun come up. Either that or let me fall asleep somehow. Or die. Get *off* me! Slap.

There was really no protection from the bugs or the enemy. I clutched my M-16, never took my hands off it once. I just lay there and tried to sleep somehow. Every half hour the guy on the left would bump the guy to his right, and eventually it came around to me—not that I'd been able to nod off, not for one second. I felt so alone. It was one-thirty in the morning, we were served up on a platter for the VC, and everyone else was sleeping. It was up to me to stay alert and watch for something moving in the darkness even though it was so dark it would be impossible to see anything anyway.

I got through the half hour. It wasn't difficult to stay awake because I was terrified. I bumped the guy on my right and woke him up, and thought, well, I can go to sleep now. I knew I wouldn't have to wake up for at least another two or three hours. I couldn't sleep though. Good thing. I looked to my right and he was sound asleep!

I was petrified. "You can't sleep!" I whispered, as loud as I could without being too loud. "You can't sleep!" And then, "You're going to get us all killed!"

But it was no use. Whenever I pulled listening post or ambush patrol from then on, it was an all-nighter. There would be no sleeping. If the guy next to you dozed off, it was one thing. You had to hope nothing happened in those thirty minutes. But of course, he's not awake to wake the next guy up, and pretty soon there's no ambush patrol. There are just eight dead soldiers.

I hadn't been out in the field one week when it started to register what kind of hell I'd signed up for. Vietnam was one thing. But Vietnam on no sleep? I might as well shoot myself, I thought, and save the VC the trouble.

CHAPTER 2

The Darkest Night

The Far Side didn't appear in newspapers for another decade, but Gary Larson nailed Vietnam in one frame. One guy sits bolt upright in bed, and the guy in the next bunk tries to calm him down. The entire room is engulfed in flames. "Go back to sleep, Chuck," the sane one says. "You're just having a nightmare." Pause. "Of course, we are still in hell."

We were in hell, but we got used to it, and the days started to go by. Time went fast, really, which surprised me. The only time it slowed to a stop was when I wrote letters, especially to my girlfriend. I could get to feeling quite sorry for myself, wondering what she was up to and whether she was waiting for me after all.

Mostly though, I found myself—unbelievably—counting my blessings. I'm not kidding. I was happy to be with a mech outfit because I didn't have to walk. Out of the entire 25th Division, there were only two mech outfits—mechanized, with all the big guns. There was mine, the 4th of the 23rd, and then an outfit we called the Triple Deuce, the 2nd of the 22nd. The rest were leg outfits, so most people were legs.

It's funny. The guys in the leg outfits were generally glad they were in them. They didn't want to be like me, on top of a big track. The biggest guns, after all, drew the most fire. You hit an anti-tank mine and the entire thing would blow up, killing everyone on it. Granted the foot soldiers couldn't see the booby traps, but you could fall into a punji pit and probably still live, or trip a grenade and have a chance at living. If you're sitting on top of a track and get hit with a rocket-propelled grenade, no way. I suppose it's why some people are afraid to fly. Statistically you're more likely to die in an automobile crash, but it still feels safer on the ground. If you're in the air and things go wrong, well, you know.

I've never been afraid of flying, and being on a track didn't scare me. I was reckless that way, I suppose. I just didn't think it would be my APC getting hit—the invincibility of youth and all. Whatever it was, I was glad I didn't have to walk. You had to carry everything if you were walking. Guys in the leg outfits carried their M-16 and ammunition, C rations, anything they'd sleep in—like their shelter halfs or blankets—clothes, cigarettes, you name it. It was backbreaking.

I'd look at the leg outfits, and think, "No thanks." It's like what they say: if everyone sitting around a table put their problems in the middle of it, you'd probably take yours back. Whatever danger you felt, it was the one you were used to, and whatever anyone else was dealing with seemed worse. Not only that, but every day that went by without my getting killed only reinforced my illusion that I would never be. I started to feel charmed, believe it or not.

Oh sure, reality slapped me hard across the face once in a while. I'll never forget the first time I was near where any of our men were killed. The mech outfits were occasionally called on to help the legs, and toward the end of October we were called to help a leg outfit called the Wolfhounds. They had a man missing from a nasty firefight, and we were supposed to secure the area and help them find him.

The Wolfhounds were probably an hour from where we were, so a few tracks escorted the Rome plows back to the perimeter. The rest of us took off. We got the coordinates and went across country until we found them. By the time we did, the firing had stopped. We had dropped napalm on the area—it had gotten that intense. Napalm is like motor oil on fire and it wipes out everything it touches. There are no trees anymore, nothing green. There is only black. Anyone doused with napalm is going to die. It's next to impossible to even identify them, they're charred that bad.

It wasn't that long, from what I remember, before some guys from our company found the body of the missing man. I never saw him, but I wonder if the guys who did have ever recovered. It was that gruesome, or so I was told. Over the years I've heard many stories of Vietnam vets who returned from the war never to leave their house again. All I have to do is look back on this, and I understand.

We spent the night with the Wolfhounds, waiting to see if Charlie would come back. That's what we called the enemy: Viet Cong, VC, Victor Charlie, Charlie for short. Sir Charles if we were getting our asses kicked.

We figured that after the napalm was dropped they had scattered back into their tunnels, because it was a quiet night and we took no fire. Daylight came but the call from the listening post didn't. A few guys went out to find them and they were dead. We couldn't believe it. Every leg outfit had a dog, and the dog always went with on listening post.

Apparently all three guys on LP had fallen asleep. I wasn't so surprised to hear that. I could imagine thinking, well, the dog will smell Charlie and you'd have that warning. Could the dog have fallen asleep, too? It must have, because its throat had been slit just like each of the men.

The listening post was never that far from where we were at

the time, in this case probably a couple of football fields from the perimeter. If something was going wrong, we figured we would have heard it. But if you cut someone's jugular they can't scream, their vocal chords are severed. So somehow Charlie got to the dog first, then the men.

I couldn't sleep on listening post before and now I was damn sure I never would. I guess I never realized you could die out there like that. I could imagine a firefight, but for them to sneak up on you and slit your throat before you knew what was happening, that was hard to process.

So I did what I was learning to do. I just moved on. Nobody talked about what had happened or what they saw. We moved on.

It was time to leave the area, and as the APCs rolled by a cemetery we stopped our track. "What are you doing?" I hollered out to a Wolfhound who was digging up graves. He was using an entrenching tool in this cemetery, which was very old, and I couldn't understand what the hell he thought he was up to. "I'm digging for a body count," he hollered back. "You're shitting me," I yelled. "These graves are a hundred years old!" He may have been finding VC in there, but so what? There weren't any fresh bodies, and I thought he was nuts.

This was his justification. Our senior commander in Vietnam, General William Westmoreland, wanted seven dead VC for every dead American. We had three dead Americans, so now we needed twenty-one dead VC. So this guy was saying, okay, here's a body. His commander had told him he had to find bodies, but apparently he hadn't elaborated. You'd think that if he would count bodies from a century ago, it wouldn't bother him to just lie to the CO to begin with. I thought it was a stupid way to keep track of whether we were winning or losing, and to this day I do not trust a single statistic coming out of the war.

The VC were on to us when it came to body counts. They

would drag their dead away and bury them in the walls of their tunnels so we couldn't get a count. We found blood and whatever else, but it was rare that we recovered bodies—from what I saw anyway—unless they had to leave in a hurry. As far as our men, we weren't concerned about the count so much as what they would do to their bodies.

The VC didn't drag off the bodies of our soldiers. They hung them in trees after they mutilated them or found some other way to haunt us with them. Our troops weren't above making a statement, though. One reason my memories of the Wolfhounds are so vivid is that when some killed a VC, they cut the ears off and hung them on their belts as trophies.

Not every battle was against the enemy, of course. We pulled stupid shit, too. The guy who was driving my APC for a while was a real smart-ass. He was black, and when his hand got blown off in a shotgun cleaning accident, he claimed it was a race thing.

Now usually out of seven guys on my track, at least three of them were black. It would have been stupid to get on someone because of their race, even if we would have been inclined, which we weren't. Half the time we would have been outnumbered.

Every night we had thousand-gallon rubber tires flown in with fuel. One was gas and one was diesel, but not very many APCs ran on gas. One night this guy decided he didn't want to wait in line for the diesel because that's the kind of person he was. He topped the APC off with gas, so the next morning when we fired it up it ran hot.

That was the last time he drove the APC.

He was forever trying to pick fights with different guys, who began to wonder whose side he was on. "Christ," someone finally said. "Why would I fight you? You're a Golden Glove. You'd knock the shit out of me." Didn't we have enough problems without fighting each other? He was not a happy man, so when he had to go back into base camp because he had lost his hand, we all thought good riddance.

A guy named Poncho started driving our track after that.

We were still clearing the jungle, still in the Ho Bo Woods, in the Filhol Rubber Plantation. There was a lot to worry about besides land mines or sniper fire. We had B-52 air strikes almost every day. It was called carpet bombing. The bombs would leave huge craters, each about the size of a house. In fact there'd be water in them during the monsoons, and some of us swam in them—that's how big they were.

Sometimes the trees we pushed down with Rome plows covered those holes, and the APC drivers coming up behind had no way of knowing there wasn't ground underneath. They'd start driving over a hole, break the trunks of the trees, and the entire track would fall in.

Tree stumps were also a hazard. It didn't matter how closely you were paying attention. Shit happened.

Of course, paying attention helped. Poncho didn't on a couple of occasions and it cost him. He drove the track into a tree stump. Since his head was sticking out of that little round opening in the top of the track, it hit the steel and his lip busted wide open. The rest of us flew off the APC, but weren't injured seriously. Poncho had to be medevac'd out. Clark had me fill in as driver for the couple of days he was gone. Only days later, he did the exact same thing. This time he was laid up in the hospital so long we lost track of him.

Poncho had been driving the lead track at the time, track 23. I had helped him drive a few times when he got tired. So after he got hurt, Clark asked me if I'd drive. Sure, I said. I thought it was a great deal, actually. I got first pick of the C rations and I didn't have to go on listening post or ambush patrol anymore because as a driver, I had to be alert. I also got the first and last shifts on the TC hatch at night, which meant that, of anyone, I got the most uninterrupted sleep. You can't believe how much that meant to me.

I knew there were risks. The lead track would be the first to hit an antitank mine, after all. And it wasn't until I got back from Vietnam that I learned that Cu Chi was considered the most dangerous piece of real estate in the world—one of the most dangerous jobs in Vietnam, in probably the most dangerous spot. But my choice of C rations! And better sleep. That was too tempting to pass up. It never even occurred to me to say no. Sure, I'd drive. I'd drive lead.

And days went by. We continued to escort the Rome plows, clearing more woods. Every once in a while a plow or track would hit a butterfly bomb. Those are just mines that are dropped from the air, with little fins that rotate like a helicopter blade. The fins slow their descent so they don't blow up when they land. That happens later, when a track runs over them.

One bright, hot, sunny day, probably one o'clock in the afternoon, I heard this thud. Nothing too unusual about that. Our track had hit something, that was all. Les Cowden, our medic and another Minnesota boy (he was from Anoka) was riding with me. I thought it was a butterfly bomb, but he thought it was more than that. He jumped off the track and dug until he found the canister. It was two or three hundred pounds! Just the detonator had gone off, so we'd been lucky. If it had functioned properly it would have blown our track to smithereens.

I thought, oh my God, if that thing would have blown, there would have been nothing left of any of us. It spooked me, what could have been. This thing hadn't shaken the track at all. It had been in the ground for so long the explosives didn't work anymore.

It was so odd that Cowden jumped off. Nobody ever jumped off the track when something like that happened. You heard a bang and just kept going.

It struck me how random it all was. And for a long time, there was no such thing as a routine thud or bang. I stayed jittery for days. That was Vietnam: long stretches of boredom punctuated by bouts of terror.

I turned twenty that November, but what stands out about the month was Thanksgiving. They flew dinner out to us at noon, by helicopter. I couldn't believe how good it was. The meal was so fancy it included a menu. First an appetizer of shrimp and crackers. Then roast turkey—even white meat—with mashed potatoes and gravy, cornbread dressing, and cranberry sauce. There were hot rolls with butter, candy, nuts and relishes, fresh fruit, even pumpkin pie with whipped topping.

I piled my plate as high as I could, and with no offense to my mother or wife, I dug into a feast that tasted better than anything I had had before or would since. Oh sure, a couple of months of lima beans in a can and it wouldn't have taken much to impress, but still. It was incredible.

I sat up on a little knoll by myself and ate. For once there was some time to reflect. Of course I thought about what my family and my girlfriend were doing back home, all gathered around their little Norman Rockwell holiday tables. I didn't feel sorry for myself, though, not one bit. I was too stunned by the bounty right in front of me.

Granted there would be no nap, no leftovers, no football on TV. But life was temporarily as good as it got in Vietnam, and I was very thankful. I was sleeping better than I had since my first day in the field and I had my choice of C rations, all because I was driving the APC. That's it! That's what I was thankful for. I was thankful that Poncho whacked his lip on the track and had to go to the hospital.

I have spent the last thirty-seven years wondering what happened during the next few weeks, and I still can't tell you. It was up north, deeper into the Iron Triangle, and we were helping a leg outfit with the 1st Infantry Division. That's all I remember. In my letters home all I wrote was something to the effect that it wasn't very nice where we were. You weren't supposed to give your location or name anyone in your letters in case they fell into the wrong hands. We heard stories of how the VC intercepted mail and wrote to the return address, saying whoever it was had been killed and giving all sorts of bogus but gory details that terrorized their families.

There are techniques you can use to refresh memories that have been suppressed. I've never been tempted to refresh anything where these few weeks were concerned.

I do remember coming back into base camp on Christmas Eve. The company welcomed us "home" with ribbons of smoke in different colors, and a trailer full of pop and beer on ice. I had a beer, watched a movie, and went back to the hooch for bed.

That was my Christmas.

A day or two later I helped set up for Bob Hope. He was coming in right after Christmas, and our base camp at Cu Chi was just one of his stops. We put up the stage, set up all the chairs, and looked forward to the show. Toward evening our CO told us it was time to pull security for the perimeter.

Huh? I mean, granted this was Vietnam and orders changed quickly and you never knew what you were going to be doing from one minute to the next, but he had to have been kidding. You have us set up for a show and then not let us see it?

Turns out only the housecats—that's what we called the people stationed at base camp, the clerk-typists and anyone else with an office job—got to be in the audience. They wanted a lot of security for Bob Hope, and I understood that. But to not let the guys who were actually fighting the war see him? That didn't make sense to me. Clark happened to be at base camp at the time and could have gone, but he didn't. He was protesting. I would have, too, but I was a mile away—on watch. We didn't hear a thing that night. No enemy fire and no one-liners.

It was just as well. Why forget for one moment that you're in hell? It only made it that much worse when you came to. The 101st Airborne had moved in next to us by now, and we were supposed to help them out. They were a cocky bunch. "We're going to win this fucking war," they kept saying, like everything rested in their hands.

The guys in the 101st were getting paid extra for being jumpers. The thing was, there really weren't very many places to jump in Vietnam with all the dense vegetation, but maybe that's just my disdain talking. I sensed these guys were trouble.

Sure enough, it was only their second night in country when we were still in base camp for Christmas that we got called to help them. It was the middle of the night and they'd just gone on patrol a few miles out. They had drawn fire and retreated back.

They had also left a man behind.

Our CO gave us the word. We jumped on our tracks to go out and try to find the guy. Apparently he'd gotten lost. They assumed he was still alive, but how would they know? It didn't sound like they'd tried very hard to find him. They had just left him out there and had gone back into base camp.

What happened next is the subject of disagreement among people I still keep in touch with. One person says we found the guy alive, wounded, but alive. Another person says we found him dead, propped up against a tree—with his ears and nose and genitals cut off, and anything that would fit in his mouth stuck there.

Things like that happened. Whether it was the outcome this time, I doubt we will ever know for sure. It's like what they say about car accidents. Three different eyewitnesses to the same event, which happened minutes earlier, will have three completely different stories. Take the horror that is war, add almost forty years, and mix it with equal parts blocking out and bravado and there's no telling where you'll end up. Whatever went down wasn't pretty, because my friends and I remember the next day the same way.

I was the first to light into the others the next morning. "You don't leave men behind!" I snarled. The rage had been building overnight, and I made no attempt to hold it back. I don't remember what their reasoning was, but this was not the way you did business in Vietnam. You did not leave a man behind. You made a vow that the entire platoon would perish before that happened. The 101st Airborne apparently did not get it and had no interest in getting it. There was a fistfight, and the slightest bit of tension was released before we all calmed down a little bit. I think we had an understanding after that, but I wasn't counting on anything. I was too consumed by the horror of it all. Let's say he had been butchered. It seems to me he had been shot in the head. Hopefully if they got to him he'd saved the last bullet for himself, like they told you to do in orientation. But I didn't know, and I was fairly sure I would never recover from the experience.

I could spend the rest of my life trying and never figure out how one human being can do that to another. Doesn't matter if it happened on this particular night. It happened over there. As for the Iron Triangle, if I remember some of this but still block out those three weeks, I'm guessing we are all better off not knowing.

I distracted myself from what was happening by doing what you might expect a twenty-year-old to do. I raised hell myself, though a much more benign variety. Fast cars were important to me then—they still are—so I was determined that my APC be faster than the old man's. I got our mechanic, Dick Godbout, to take care of that. He set my track up so it was two or three miles an hour faster than the CO's. He climbed inside the old man's track and I drove mine and we raced around the motor pool. Yeah. A couple of thirteen-ton APCs and we were drag racing with them. It was difficult to get them up to even forty miles an hour, but considering how big they were I was happy.

We were still stationed at base camp. The entire camp was fifteen hundred acres and we had plenty of room to tear around. Nobody said much about it. We got away with just about everything in Vietnam. It wasn't like boot camp that way. Nobody gave us much in the way of crap, not that we would have taken it had they tried.

By now we were road running, pulling security for convoy runs coming out of Saigon. The trucks were bringing guns and ammunition and other supplies to troops south. The VC would have loved to choke off the route we were guarding, Highway One. It was just a one-lane dirt road, but it was the main artery for supplies at the time.

Godbout volunteered to go road running with us the night of December 29, 1967. He wouldn't have had to; he wasn't infantry, after all, he was a mechanic. He was going to take the mechanic's track out that night because he couldn't get the track he was working on going again. We ate supper at the mess hall together and sat there for the next few hours, talking. Everyone left after a while and it was just him and me. The evening stands out because even the guys on your track weren't usually close personal friends or anything. You might talk to them off and on all day for days at a time, but not about anything that really mattered—certainly not a whole lot about their personal life.

My conversation with Dick Godbout was different. He was pouring his heart out about how much he missed his wife. He also had a bad feeling about this particular night. It made me wonder why he'd volunteered to go along, but I didn't say anything. Don't worry about it, was all I offered. This was no big deal. I wasn't used to having guys admit they were frightened. But I'm sure that had I been, my answer would have always been the same. Don't worry about it. This is no big deal. I really had convinced myself that there was such a thing as routine duty. Looking back, it was just a way of coping. I refused to believe anything could happen to my friends or to me.

We left at the usual time, probably about ten o'clock that night, maybe ten-thirty. The runs were always in the middle of the night. The tracks had lights on them but we couldn't run with the lights on at night for obvious reasons. We ran the tracks really close together, and that by itself was dangerous—driving that close, literally bumper to bumper, at fifteen to twenty miles an hour. If one track stopped short you'd have one hell of a mess. I don't remember that ever happening, though it was pretty common for drivers to take corners too fast and throw guys off the track. No one got seriously hurt, but they'd be pissed. You just went flying.

I was using the extended laterals on my track. Laterals are the steering levers on an APC. Extended laterals were steel pipes that slipped over the laterals and came up through the hole where my head usually stuck out. They, along with a pipe that was connected to the footfeet, enabled me to sit on top of the APC and drive it from there. Mostly I used extended laterals when we were driving on roads. Charlie would sneak in and throw mines on the road, and since I was in the lead I'd be the first to hit one.

Sitting on top of the track gave you the added protection of another 3½ inches of steel. You were more vulnerable in terms of small arms fire, but you were in a much better position if you hit a mine.

I can't remember how many tracks we took out that night, but I think it was at least seven. Godbout was in the TC hatch of track 51, which was about halfway back in the pack.

We headed north, as usual, and passed two villages before getting into position. There were villagers around, so we didn't really worry about VC being in the area. When Charlie moved in, the villagers usually moved out. If we came upon an empty village, we knew there'd be a firefight. No one expected one that night. There were people all over the place, and you could see them because they were right alongside the road. The kids were there, too, with their hands out as they always were, waiting for the C rations we'd throw to them.

So much for Godbout's feeling, I thought. We weren't going to get hit that night.

We set up outside the second village. We put half the tracks on one side of the road and half on the other—into the ditches, out of the way. By now it was going on midnight. The convoy run wasn't due to pass through until about one o'clock in the morning. Godbout was on the track right next to me because when we pulled off the road, every other APC went to the other side.

The convoy came through when we expected, about one, maybe two o'clock. There were probably twelve units, many of them what we called deuce-and-a-half trucks: two-and-a-half-ton trucks carrying food, supplies, and ammunition. There were also a few tanker trucks hauling water. And it was dusty, I remember that. Dust was flying everywhere.

We were just there to keep the VC from shooting at them,

sitting ducks that they were. That's why they ran in the middle of the night, with no lights. We weren't their only protection, of course. They had radio contact if they drew any kind of fire, and within minutes we'd have gunship helicopters helping out.

It probably only took them five or ten minutes to move through, and now it was time to get back onto the road and return to camp. I got on the radio and asked the old man if I should get in the lead. Nah, he said, we were just going to go back into base camp. So we turned around, and whoever was driving the last track was now first. Godbout's track was right in front of mine.

We passed through the first small village with our lights off and drew some small-arms fire. Nothing serious, though. No one was hurt. We kept moving.

The ping, ping, ping of sniper fire pounded away at us, but we never even slowed down. I imagine a few guys probably fired back a few rounds, but we continued on our way.

As we approached the second village I noticed my track couldn't have been more than about ten yards from Godbout's. His was right on the edge of the wood line of the second village.

We drove on.

Then out of nowhere, the explosion. There was a huge flash right where Godbout was sitting and before the sound caught up with the light, Godbout was gone. He was killed right in front of me and I watched it happen. I knew right away it was an RPG-7, a rocket-propelled grenade. Oh my God, I thought, there can't be anything left of him, there just can't.

I didn't realize, with the bedlam that ensued, that three other guys were killed right behind him with the same round.

I couldn't have known what was happening in Godbout's hometown of Goffstown, New Hampshire, at that moment. It was two o'clock in the afternoon on the east coast of the United

States—there's a twelve-hour time difference between there and Vietnam—and Godbout's mother felt her heart being ripped out of her chest.

Hell continued to break loose. The old man screamed into our headsets: "Get the tracks in a line!!" As soon as you draw fire like that, you get on line, and we were supposed to pull off the road and line up outside the trees and just blast into the village.

But my track wouldn't move! The other APCs were getting into position as guys fired away, but my track was frozen and I didn't know why. The CO was still screaming in my headset and the explosions were still deafening. I kept hitting the footfeet and nothing moved. "The engine must have died!" I thought to myself, so I jumped down inside the track to figure out what the hell was wrong. The engine was running. Still in a panic, I discovered a nut had fallen off the pipe connected to the footfeet. I wasn't going to take the time to find it in a crossfire, let alone try to thread it back onto the bolt. So I took the extended laterals and the footfeet extension and tossed them all out into the ditch.

Looking back, it's amazing how quickly I got rid of those things. You move fast when you're scared shitless.

At one point I literally pinched my right leg just to make sure I was still alive. That's the honest-to-God truth. It was sheer terror. I'd always heard RPG-7 rounds were so bad you'd never even know what hit you—and I was so out-of-my-mind frightened I didn't know if I was alive or dead.

I got into position as fast as I could—it was probably within two or three minutes—and waited. The driver has to stay with the track, and in my case I was inside of it now because I didn't have the extended laterals anymore. I was somewhat glad to be inside, but if you're inside with an RPG-7 rocket on its way that's not the best place to be. Our guys were still blasting away like crazy. We had more than a dozen RPG-7 rockets shot at us that night, at least from what we discovered later.

I could see out, but the way the bullets were flying I didn't look out very often. My life didn't flash before my eyes or anything like that, even though I thought I was going to die. As most combat vets will tell you, when you're in the heat of battle all you think about is staying alive, however you can do that. Though I was also thinking, damn, I wish I wasn't a track driver so I could get out of this. I couldn't though. I was one of the sitting ducks. I had made my choice.

The rounds kept flying and I thought, oh my God, how many times can they miss? They kept shooting RPG-7s at the tracks and the tanks, trying to take out the big guns—me. What a stupid shit I am, I thought, to have ever considered this a good deal.

A couple guys came running back to the track to get more ammunition and one of them hollered at me, trying to figure out what to do about another guy who was frozen out there. "He's just lying there! He can't move! What do I do?"

I didn't know, but I had to think of something. "Remember the old John Wayne movies?" I said. "Try hittin' him with the butt of your M-16! Maybe he'll come out of it!" That's what he did and the guy came to—though of course I didn't find that out until later.

We were only five or six miles out of base camp, so the Cobra helicopters that were called in got there right away; I think there were three of them. One was hovering right over my head. It couldn't have been twenty feet above me. It felt good to have them there. Oh, it felt good. They put out so much firepower, it helped calm me down enough to start breathing again. Once they arrived and started firing I think the whole thing was over within five more minutes. The entire fight probably lasted twenty minutes, though I really have no idea.

I don't remember feeling anything at the moment Godbout died. Not at all. I'd probably gotten to know him better in three hours than I had anyone else in three months, but something inside me had shut down weeks ago, and I could have sworn I didn't feel a thing. This wasn't a good time to feel. This was a good time to panic.

After it was quiet again, we sat around and waited for daylight. That's when we went in and tried to find bodies. I think we were assigned so many dead out of that deal, too. I don't know how many we killed. A couple hours before we pulled out we saw villagers carrying the bodies of civilians who'd been killed in the crossfire. "Number ten GI," they kept saying. "Number ten GI." Government Issue. American Soldiers. Number one GI meant you were the best there is, and number ten was the worst.

It wasn't VC who got us that night. It was North Vietnamese regulars, who usually didn't tangle with us unless they really had their shit together. They were set up to take us out. If they would have actually hit us with every RPG-7 rocket they had that night, they would have. They would have wiped us out. That was the plan.

They missed a lot of their targets because it was so dark and we were moving. You try to hit a moving target at night with no lights on—I mean, a 13½-ton APC is a pretty easy mark, but at night it's not so easy, and if it's moving it's almost impossible depending on how far away you are.

Our guys had taken a few POWs overnight and there was one of them by my track. The Vietnamese interpreter assigned to our company was slapping him around, trying to get more information about what had happened the night before. The bodies of the men we had lost had been hauled off by then, and we'd gotten word that not only had four men been killed, but another had lost his leg and four more had been seriously wounded.

We went back to base camp about two o'clock and had the rest of the afternoon off. I wrote my girlfriend a letter and told her I had lost a good friend.

Clark had been working at base camp and it was his job to identify bodies. He told me Godbout took the RPG-7 round—which will penetrate 21½ inches of solid steel—right in his stomach. Clark said it looked like he had just gone to sleep. There was nothing on his face at all, no blood, nothing.

One of the other men who was killed, a Missouri boy named Scott Cook, only had one hunk of shrapnel in his eye—but it killed him instantly.

And that was it. That was the extent of any discussion.

No one said another word.

CHAPTER 3

Fifteen Minutes to Life

We never talked about the guys who died. Never. Once they were dead, that was it. There was no service, no minister, nothing. We just went on. We made a point of not talking about them. I think the feeling was that if you thought too much about death, it would consume you, and you would be next.

I couldn't stop thinking about Dick Godbout on the morning of January 8, 1968.

His death haunted me because he knew it was coming. He knew he was going to die. We had talked for a long time earlier that evening, and he just had this feeling he wasn't going to get home. He wanted to get home to see his wife. "I have a bad feeling about this one, Jon," he kept saying. And within six hours, he was dead.

That's when everything changed for me. I started worrying about things I had never worried about before. When the CO asked me to drive the 59½–ton tank I asked him what had happened to the guy who had been driving it—"Did he rotate back, or what?" The commander said no, he'd been killed the night before. "Then no thanks," I told him. I didn't want any part of that. It was the first time I'd turned down an assignment. Until then I had thought that if the bullet had your number on it, that was it. No sense worrying about it.

I didn't want to drive the 59½–ton tank because it was sort of the lead of the lead. There were two of them, and each had a 105 howitzer barrel on top of it. The big gun stuck out so far it would get hung up in the trees, so they never made the first pass through the jungle. That was the APC's job.

Suddenly I figured that driving lead APC was bad enough. It was one of the most dangerous assignments in Vietnam. Lead drivers were usually wounded or killed in thirty days or fewer, though I didn't know that at the time. And remember, I actually considered it a good deal. No more listening post and no more ambush patrol because as a driver, you had to be alert. Plus I got my choice of C rations. That was important.

There was even a day when I wasn't going to be lead APC anymore and I let the opportunity pass. The senior squad leader for my outfit, Clark, was set to go back to base camp for the remainder of his tour. The plan was that another track would then be lead, with someone else driving. "Jon," that guy asked almost as soon as he found out, "would you ever switch with me?" He had forty-five days left and wanted to go home. "I just don't want to be the lead," he said.

Well, what the hell, I thought. I'd already been driving lead anyway, so what was the difference? I really didn't think too much about it. Make that, I *tried* not to think too much about it. I felt sorry for the guy because he was afraid. "Sure," I told him. "I'll switch."

Now that worried me.

A lot of guys had a bad feeling about our new CO, Captain Lamb. He was a real gung ho type who volunteered us for all the most dangerous jobs out there. The word on him was that he was going to get us killed.

I tried not to think about that. I tried not to think about a bullet with my number. I tried not to think about Godbout. But every time I managed to put something out of my mind, something else replaced it.

There was a superstition that guys who traded in their boots were either going to get wounded or killed. I needed new boots when we were back at base camp for Christmas, so I got a pair. I never considered doing otherwise. Now I couldn't stop thinking about the boots.

Then there was my lucky piece of shrapnel. I had been hit in the chest when we were going through a cemetery, trying to advance on some VC who were firing at us. I was moving to the front between the tombstones and I felt this thump. "Damn!" I thought. "I'm wounded!" I hadn't felt the round, never even heard it. But that's how guys always said it would happen. You wouldn't feel or hear a thing. You'd just feel wet. I didn't dare look down. I just stood there for what seemed like forever, and eventually I realized I didn't feel wet. Maybe I hadn't been hit after all.

I looked down and no lie, there was a hunk of shrapnel about the size of a fifty-cent piece sticking out of my shirt. It was cool in the morning so I still had a shirt on under my flak jacket. I always left the jacket open, and the shrapnel had tapped my chest right over my heart. It was just hanging there. It had all these jagged edges and was obviously part of a hand grenade. My lucky piece, I decided. To have been hit with something that big and not get hurt—that was something.

I carried it in my pocket from then on. It was my security blanket for weeks. One day I lost it, probably when I was changing shirts. I wasn't one to get upset about much, and certainly not something this minor, but it bothered me a lot. I wrote to Darlene about it: that's how much it got to me.

I tried not to think about Godbout, I tried not to think

about the boots, and I tried not to think about my lucky piece of shrapnel. For that matter I tried not to think about my dad, who had cried twice in his life that I knew of—once on the day I left for Vietnam. Suddenly that worried me. I wondered if he knew something I didn't.

I had done my best to reassure Godbout that what we were up to the night he died was no more dangerous than anything else we did routinely. Now I knew better. It was dangerous, much more so than working with the Rome plows. I hoped.

I told myself that road running was more dangerous, and now things could get back to normal. We were back to pulling security for the Rome plows, like we'd been doing day after day for months. I just wanted things to get back to normal, and working with the Rome plows felt like that. The morning of January 8, 1968, felt normal. Comforting even. I just wanted back into our routine. I don't remember what day of the week this was. We never thought in terms of that, it was just days left in our tour: 265 in my case.

I was so glad to be back with the Rome plows on this particular morning I didn't even worry about the sandbags. The night before I'd taken all the sandbags out of the APC to be replaced with new ones. The floor of the track was 3½ inches of steel, but we put sandbags on top of it for more protection against shrapnel. You had to replace them every so often because they'd break. These were in bad shape, and after I tossed them I bailed sand out of the bottom of the track. But it got dark before I could get new ones in there. Once night fell, you couldn't see anything at all, so that was it. I didn't really worry about it, though. If something could penetrate 3½ inches of steel I doubted sandbags were going to help much.

I wasn't worried about not having the extended laterals either. Remember, extended laterals let you drive on top of the APC, and instead of just 3½ inches of steel on the floor of the track you had 3½ inches of steel on the top, too. It helped protect you from mines. I wasn't as worried about mines anymore, not after what had happened to Dick. I just didn't want to be on top of the track.

We pulled out for the day at seven, as usual, and I was driving inside the track because I didn't have the laterals. The first thing I heard on the radio was the CO asking me where they were. "They're back in the ditch where we got in that firefight on Road One," I told him. "The night Godbout was killed I got caught in the crossfire and the footfeet fell off."

"God!" the CO said, pissed. "You should have them!"

I didn't respond. It was time for me to break trail for the first cut.

"Delta 22," the CO said a moment later. "Pull around the two tanks and make a hard left into the jungle."

Before I could even pull alongside the first tank, that was it.

I went from 265 days left, to zero.

My track had hit an antitank mine. Its six-cylinder Chrysler diesel engine broke through a two-inch solid steel cover like it was wet toilet paper and landed fifty yards away. Darrell Dyer from my squad was sitting on a two-by-eight board in the TC hatch and was blown straight up in the air, hitting the board so hard with his ass on the way back down that he broke it in half. The rest of the guys were blown off the track except for me and another guy.

"Where's Hovde?" Cowden, the medic, hollered. "He's inside the track!" someone hollered back. Cowden saw smoke and flames coming out of the hole where I'd been sitting. His hair caught fire when he pulled me out of it. Somehow they got that put out while he took my pulse. He knew right away my left leg was gone. He pulled me out of the hole and the leg didn't follow. It was still inside the track.

He let go of my hand. "Hovde's dead," he said.

The CO was calling for the dustoff helicopters by now and Darrell was standing in front of the APC. The tanks were starting to move so they could set up a perimeter with the dustoffs coming in. Cowden was heading for another injured soldier when suddenly something scared the shit out of Darrell. "Les!" he screamed. "Hovde just moved!"

Cowden rushed back and took my pulse again. This time it happened to be in my other arm. "He's alive!" he said. Turns out my left arm had been severed just below the elbow but was still in my shirtsleeve. I was losing so much blood Cowden doubted I'd make it, but there was no way he was giving up. By now the helicopter pilot had radioed in to find out if the area had been secured. "It's not," the CO radioed back, "but if you don't come in right now we have one man that ain't going to make it."

It took five guys to load me onto the helicopter. Len McLean was one of them. He was trying to stop the bleeding and thread an IV into my right arm but I was fighting it. I kept trying to get up. Decades later he remembers this very vividly. He finally got the IV in me and said that little bit of stump on my left leg kept coming up at him. "I can still see that stump," he recalled. Maybe it was a reflex, I don't know. But it was one hellacious ride to the 12th Evacuation Hospital, even for someone like Len, who was used to the worst.

There weren't any tourniquets in the field, so McLean had used arm slings instead. That's the first thing they wanted to know when I got to the operating room fifteen minutes after the APC hit the mine—why he hadn't used tourniquets. "I don't have any!" he told them. They got him stocked up and told him thanks, he could go now.

Oh, and Hovde's not going to make it.

He just stood there for a moment taking that in when a

nurse hollered at him and asked if he was wounded. She was good looking, really filled out her fatigues. He looked down. Until that moment he hadn't realized how soaked he was in my blood. "Uh," he said. "Yeah." He hoped by the time she made it over to him he'd have figured out a way to change his story smoothly enough to get a date. Instead she hollered at an older, heavyset nurse to help him out. "Oh," he told that one, "I guess I'm okay."

I lost my left arm just above the elbow. The arm they saved, my right arm, had 175 stitches in it and was in a cast. My right leg was in a cast, too—185 stitches in that—and it was broken. The bone was sticking right out of the skin from what I was told. Plus my foot was so badly crushed it looked like scrambled eggs. My stumps were packed in gauze and wrapped with tight Ace bandages. There was string running out of each one that went through a pulley system with four or five pounds of weight to keep the skin from recessing back into my body. I only had about 4½ inches of leg on the left side. My right arm was busted at the wrist, and my fingers were broken in so many places they couldn't save the middle one. They sewed the index finger back on, but it looks funny to this day. My middle finger was gone below the first knuckle. It was difficult to believe, but I had no internal injuries—though I did take a piece of shrapnel near my eye. There were IVs on both sides of my groin, and tubes running everywhere. They were giving me blood, morphine, everything. I was a mess. No arm, no leg, and the rest of me looked like I'd been through a blender.

No one could believe I was still alive.

When I woke up six days later, I didn't want to be. I wanted to die. I knew right away I'd lost an arm and a leg, but that wasn't it. Everything hurt so much. God it hurt. It felt like there was a lightning bolt running through my leg—except a lightning bolt would have stopped. This didn't. I could not imagine getting through another minute of it, let alone a lifetime. I just kept screaming in agony.

There was a high-ranking officer next to my bed when I came to. He said something about my service to the country and pinned a Purple Heart on my pillow. He didn't stay long.

The first thing I wanted was a mirror because my face felt so hot. My nurse, Kay Layman, got one right away. I didn't look like a white man, I'll tell you that. "They're not deep burns," she said, softly. "They won't scar. They'll clear up soon." It helped a lot to know that. If I would have had a mangled face on top of everything else I think I would've given up right then. Months later when I was recovering at Letterman General Hospital in San Francisco, I got to know another vet whose face was just a hideous mass of scar tissue. His mother and wife refused to believe it was him when they visited for the first time and they never came back. Next thing I knew the guy got a weekend pass to see friends who lived on an upper floor of a high-rise and he took the opportunity to jump out their window and be done with it.

I felt very lucky to still have my face.

Nurse Kay gave me a summary of my injuries and then said there were a couple of guys who wanted to see me. "You're not going to be awake very long," she said. "We're going to give you another heavy dose of morphine." I nodded.

I looked up, and there was the guy who had asked me to switch with him so he wouldn't have to drive lead. Tears were streaming down his face. That got to me, because you never saw guys cry in Vietnam. "My God, Jon," he said, "it should be me in that bed and not you."

I looked at him. "Don't do this," I said. "Don't you dare go through the rest of your life thinking that. If you'd been driving that day you might have been over two inches and missed the mine. That's fate."

I meant it. I never had any remorse about switching with him. Not from the minute I woke up, and not now. That was a game I refused to play. So many guys in the time since have said, "Maybe if you'd have been driving with the extended laterals you wouldn't have been hurt as badly." "Yeah?" I'll say. "How do you know my head wouldn't have been blown right off hanging over that hole?"

I didn't second-guess anything when I woke up, and I didn't feel bitter. Not then, not ever—though I did want to die from the pain and would have been happy to make any deals with God where that was concerned. Right on cue, Chaplain Donald Ostroot stepped over to my bed. "Jon," he said, "I know you're hurting. But you have to hang in there. I'm going to look you up in ten years, and you're going to be very successful and have a family. I just know that about you."

"Yeah?" I thought to myself. "Easy for you to say. You're not writhing in pain and missing half your body."

Then he said, "You're the most popular guy in the intensive care ward. You're getting about fifty cards and letters a day." I lifted my head to look at the credenza, which was covered with them. He reminded me what Nurse Kay had said, that I was only going to be awake a total of fifteen minutes—and there were only a few left. "I can read two letters," he said. "Which ones do you want me to open?"

Oh, man. I knew there would be a letter from my mom in there, and I was sure that one would be fine. I was pretty sure Darlene would have written, too, but I was much less confident about that.

"Start with my mom's," I said.

"Please come home, Jonny," Ostroot began reading. "Dad

and I are going to sleep upstairs when you get here, so you don't have to worry about the steps." My parents had a little bedroom on the main floor, and my dad never even went upstairs. The steps were narrow and steep and he just never ventured up there. Never. I bet it had been years. "Now that's love," I thought right away. There wasn't a whole lot more to the letter other than that they loved me and wanted me home, that kind of thing. But it made me feel a lot better and gave me the confidence to hear what Darlene had to say.

"If there's one from my girlfriend in there, would you read that?" I asked. My heart was pounding. This was it. If she was writing to say goodbye—and that happened to guys over here—I was prepared to give up. It may as well have been a coin toss. She wants me back, I live. She says goodbye, I say goodbye.

Ostroot started reading.

"Dear Jonny," it said, "I don't care about the amputations. I love you so much. Please come home. Nothing's changed. I still want to get married. . . ."

Life it is.

CHAPTER 4

Lucky Guy

Monday, March 15, 1999. Thirty-one years after returning from Vietnam, I logged onto the Internet and saw this e-mail:

Jon, This is going to blow your mind. I was a medic at the 12th Evac hospital when you came in. I remember you very well as you were one of "my" patients. I was tall, 6′ 3″, and wore a long handlebar mustache and glasses. Your first few dressing changes were done under general anesthetic as they were very painful procedures, and I am not sure how much of the first few days you remember as we tried to keep you pretty doped up. . . .

I remember you very well, have thought of you and many other guys often—hundreds of times—and hope all is well with you. I would also be happy to send you a picture of me as I was then if you would like to try and see if you can remember me. God bless you, Jon, and please feel free to contact me. Bruce D. Ashworth

I corresponded a lot with Bruce after that. He's a dear friend. Bruce helped me fill in details from the 12th Evac that no one else could have.

He told me they changed my dressings every twenty-four to

forty-eight hours. I don't remember anything for six days after I was wounded, but Bruce said I kept talking to people and trying to get up. It was the damnedest thing. One day he finally just asked me, "Jon, why do you keep trying to sit up?" "I just want to see what's going on," I told him in my delirium. That sounds like me.

One of the first things I do remember when I came to, January 14, 1968, was that somebody else's dog tags were next to my bed. It was eerie. It almost made me want to ask, "Where are Jon Hovde's tags? Is he dead?" You wear dog tags on a long chain around your neck, and that's how they know who you are when you come into the hospital. I'm sure they pull those off you right away, though, and somehow mine got mixed up with someone else's. I never got mine back.

Mostly what I remember is that the pain in my right leg never let up, not for one second. For the next thirty days it was brutal. The leg throbbed so bad that if someone even touched my bed I thought I'd shoot off of it. Every minute that went by I was sure I couldn't take it anymore. Morphine gave me some relief, but I slept through most of what it relieved and when it wore off I woke up and began groaning in agony once more.

I never had to ask for drugs. For the next several days they kept me as comfortable as they could—and by that I mean very sedated. It doesn't seem like they were worried about guys becoming addicts. I think in cases like mine they would have almost welcomed it, because it meant we would have survived long enough to have the problem.

Chaplain Donald Ostroot continued his watch beside my bed, as did Father J. E. Vessels. Ostroot continued reading me letters from people back home. The minute I woke up, he started in again. I had cards and letters from so many people from my hometown of Fertile and God knows where else. My uncle Loren from Long Beach had put my name in the *Los Angeles Times*, asking people to write to me at Christmas, and I was still hearing from them.

After the first couple of letters the very first time I woke up, those from my mom and Darlene, I had my will to live back. Ostroot seemed determined I wouldn't lose it. The letters helped. Though honestly all I really looked forward to during those couple of weeks was my next dose of morphine.

I always looked forward to Nurse Kay as well. She was twenty-seven then and really nice looking, though that was the last thing on my mind. I just wanted to get comfortable and she helped. She always helped. It was just this way she had, always very kind and caring.

My parents called me in the hospital not long after I woke up and I talked to them on a one-way line. That's all we had back in those days. It was kind of like our radio in the field. When you finished talking you'd say, "Over," and then the person on the other end of the line knew they could talk. My dad tried to talk to me but he kept forgetting to say "Over." "Say, 'Over,' Ole, say, 'Over!'" I could hear my mom hollering in the background. After about three exchanges like that Dad just gave up. He handed the phone to my mom and said, "You talk to him."

I had been making progress for about a week when Kay was at my bed again, but this time the look on her face was not good. "Your fever is up to 108 degrees," she said. "Your doctor has ordered you an ice blanket." I didn't even know I had a fever. My face felt hot all the time anyway from being burned. "It's serious, Jon," she said. "108 degrees is deadly."

Bruce Ashworth did the honors. The ice blanket was just an air mattress with a hose they pumped ice water through. He put my naked body on top of that, but I still had sheets on top of me along with three or four army blankets.

When they put me on that blanket the pain almost killed me

on the spot. Everything I'd been through with my leg, and suddenly the leg didn't even hurt compared to the spasms that went through me when they moved me onto the blanket—and again when they turned the ice water on.

Right away I was sure I would die, though death seemed a much kinder fate than one more minute like that. "Will you do me a favor?" I asked Kay. "Would you please wrap me in an army blanket before they put me in the body bag?" I wasn't kidding. I saw guys getting zipped into body bags all the time, because I was in the intensive care ward with the worst of the worst. It didn't scare me to die, but it scared the hell out of me to think there would be no relief from the cold. "Please just make sure I'm wrapped in a blanket," I begged.

I couldn't imagine surviving ten whole minutes that way. "How long do you think I'll be on this?" I asked, bracing myself for Kay to say, well, maybe an hour. But she wouldn't bite. "I don't know," she said. "Everyone's different. It just depends."

"Well," I pressed her, "you must have some experience with this. How long does it normally take?"

"I'm sorry, Jon," she said. "I just can't tell you."

Looking back, I can see why they wouldn't want to guess. If they said twenty-four hours and it was longer, you might die just from the disappointment.

An hour went by.

Then two.

I could not imagine anything a POW was going through that could have been worse than the agony I was in. I've had kids in audiences say that. They tell me it sounds like something they'd do to prisoners to torture them, and I agree. It was torture. You might think you'd eventually get numb and then it wouldn't be so bad, but that's not what happened. There was never any relief.

I thought of all the stories I'd heard about people with hypothermia dying a peaceful death, and I just couldn't imagine that.

There was nothing to do but shiver, and pray that you would make it through another minute. Both chaplains kept vigil, reading me letters and verses from the Bible.

Three hours.

Then four.

After it had been four hours, Kay was at my bed with more bad news. "The fever hasn't broken yet, Jon, so the doctors have ordered another blanket."

You're kidding.

"What could be more deluxe than this?" I asked, incredulous.

"It's not more deluxe, Jon," she said, patiently. "It's just another one."

"Where on earth are you going to put *that*?" I gasped.

She took a breath and told me as gently as she could. It was going on top of me. Instead of a sheet and regular blankets, I'd have an ice blanket on top of me, too.

And so I became one of the sandwich boys. That's what they called us, the wounded men in ice blankets trying to get their fevers down. Thirty-one years later, Bruce could still remember one was green and one was blue. Can you imagine? He said it was so traumatic, putting me on them, that even their colors stood out.

My right leg was cast all the way to the hip, and my right arm was cast to the shoulder. Other than that, there was nothing between me and the ice—I was literally packed in it. Not only that, but they packed three bread bags full of it and put one on each side of my head and one across the top. When they started pumping ice water through the second blanket it was as if everything inside me just collapsed in despair. "How am I ever going to survive this?" I wanted to cry.

That's all I could think. "How am I going to get through this?" It was like being in my car, naked, in the middle of a thirty-below Minnesota winter day. But at least then someone would have stopped to help. All I got was attitude from Kay when I wouldn't tell her the ice in the bags around my head had melted. "That's the only time I get a break," I protested. The ice melted and the water started to warm me up a little bit. That's how cold I was, that something so minimal could make such a difference. I was not about to give it up.

People passed by my bed constantly and they just let me freeze! To death! I grew more sure of that by the second. I was freezing to death and thinking, God, what a horrible way to die.

Kay kept changing the ice in the bags next to my head, and somehow day turned into night and back to day again. I was getting as much morphine as ever, but I wasn't sleeping. I couldn't. Even if I could have fallen asleep somehow, and God only knows how that would have been possible, I didn't want to. I was afraid that if I went to sleep I wouldn't wake up. "That's the way most guys die," Kay admitted, which scared me even more. "They give up. They go to sleep and they just never wake up."

That's probably what kept me going more than anything. All I had been through, only to die like this? No thanks.

At dawn on day two of the ice blankets, Kay greeted me by saying Tom Bailey in the next bed wanted to tell me to hang in there. "Easy for him to say," I snapped. "He's not lying here on ice blankets." "Well, Jon," she said, "he has been." She pulled one bag away from my head to put more ice in it, and I turned to look at Tom. He probably wasn't even fifteen feet from me and was missing three limbs. On his one leg part of his foot was gone, too—though I didn't find that out until later. But to this day I can still see that smile. Damned if he didn't have the biggest, brightest smile I'd ever seen on anyone, let alone anyone in Nam, let alone anyone in the ward.

If he can lose three limbs and be that freaking happy, I thought, maybe I'd better just bear down and get through this.

My doctor came in that afternoon with more bad news. "The fever's not breaking, Jon, and we don't know why. I'm afraid I missed something when you came in. I'm going to do some exploratory surgery and try to find out what's keeping the fever so high."

Then he said, "I haven't lied to a kid in Vietnam yet, and I'm not going to start with you." Pause. "You're so weak, I don't think you're going to survive the surgery."

Believe it or not, this was news I could handle. For one thing, I didn't really believe I was going to die. For another, they'd have to put me out if they were going to operate, and there would be a relief from the ice. I was euphoric. Between the promise of a little break and the new attitude I'd copped from Tom, I was my old self for a moment.

"Doc!" I hollered. "You can't kill a Norwegian and you know it."

He kind of smiled the weak smile you'd give someone on their deathbed who's joking about it, and continued on his way.

I wasn't joking. As much as I'd been through I didn't think a little exploratory surgery was going to kill me.

But it did.

Bruce was in the room, and things did not go well. He watched as they pronounced me dead and he helped prepare the death certificate.

That was going to be the end of my story, right there.

And then, the beep.

I was back.

Chaplain Vessels wrote to my parents and said my condition fluctuated too much from one day to the next to predict much of anything. "We almost lost him last night," he said, "and I have to be honest with you. By the time you get this letter you may have already heard that he's gone. That's how touch-and-go everything is at the moment."

I had slept through the night, and don't remember anything until the next morning. I woke up to see my doctor approaching the bed, all smiles. "You're right, Jon," he said right away. "Apparently you can't kill a Norwegian." He told me he couldn't find any reason why the fever shouldn't lift, adding that he thought if I could hang in with the ice blankets, I'd probably make it after all.

My heart sank. "But how much longer?" I asked. "How much longer do you think I'll need to be on them?"

He didn't know. He just couldn't tell me.

I'm a fighter, but I really didn't know how much longer I could stand it. I was getting weaker by the minute. The surgery had been a break from the unrelenting ice cold *hell*—sorry, that's the best way to describe it—but I was wiped out from it just the same. You can only fight so long before you just start wearing out, and I was wearing out.

There was nothing left to do but pray. It was time to make some deals with God. Okay, I thought, here goes. Three vows. If you get me out of this, I promise three things. One, I will have the fastest car in Polk County, Minnesota. I wasn't sure how impressed God would be with that, but I was twenty and there was no sense lying to the big guy. Two, I will not be dependent on the government. I didn't know how I was going to become a productive member of society given my amputations, but I knew I could figure that one out.

Third, I will make a difference with my life.

The first two vows popped into my head right away. The

third took a little longer, and honestly I can't say I came up with it all by myself. Remember I had two chaplains next to my bed all the time, reading me letters, but also reading from the Bible. I wouldn't be surprised if one of them had planted something like that. In fact if you read a letter one chaplain wrote to my parents, he says something about being sure my life will make a difference to thousands of people in the years to come. Wherever it came from, I was pretty sure God was going to expect more from me than a fast car and a job to make payments on it with—and this sounded as good as anything.

Ned Seachrist, a guy from my outfit who tracked me down long after the war, found this interesting. He says if you go to a King James version of the Bible and look in Jude, verse 22, you'll find a reference to having compassion and making a difference.

Once I made the vows, I was overcome with a strange sense of peace. I knew somehow I'd be okay. I really did. I quit worrying about whether I'd make it. I just had this feeling I would.

Sure enough, within a few hours Kay was at my bed to tell me the fever had broken. They didn't waste any time getting me off the ice blankets and oh, I have never been so happy in my *life*. Thank you *God*. I knew I had a lot of work ahead of me, but I also knew that nothing could be as bad as what I'd just survived.

I don't know if I have ever been as excited as the moment I knew that ordeal was over. Thirty-six years later when I relived the experience for this book, it was so traumatic it almost sent me back into shock. I woke up during the night, my bedclothes soaked in sweat. Once was enough. I was glad this part of the story was over, again.

I tell you what, if you're going to lose an arm and a leg in war you should have to spend a few days on ice blankets—if you can survive them, that is. Because you will feel like you're the luckiest person alive, even without two limbs. I swear to God. I never for one moment thought, oh, poor me. Instead I thought, I'm going to live!

That's it. That's all I could think.

I'm going to live.

I was in awe.

I spent twenty-three days at the 12th Evac, which may have been a record, I don't know. It took so long to get me stabilized. Kay noticed I was looking pretty scraggly. I never had a bath out in the field, and it's not like I let anyone touch me long enough to get in even a sponge bath in the hospital. The leg still hurt too much—not that I was groaning in agony anymore. I was too happy. "I'm going to shave you one of these days," Kay kept telling me. She never had time during the day, though, so one night she came in on her own time to do it.

She already had shaving cream on my face when she pulled out a straightedge. I looked at her. My dad used one of those, one of the old ones with a strop, and he kept the blade so sharp you could split a hair with it.

"Have you used one of those very often?" I asked, trying to sound nonchalant. "Well, no," she said. "Not really."

"God," I said, "just please don't slip with that thing in your hand." I mean, everything I'd been through and you wouldn't think the prospect of a few more stitches would faze me, but it did. To this day I can still see her coming at me with that straightedge. But it was fine. She did okay.

They kept me in the hospital for days after this to make sure the fever didn't return, but eventually my orders came. Orders to leave Vietnam: that's a big day in your life. I was getting out of there—alive. What a privilege. I was supposed to be flown to Saigon, stay there overnight, and be taken to the 106th General Hospital in Tokyo, Japan.

I'm safe now, I kept thinking. What a relief.

And what an idiot.

The night before I left I started hearing them. I kept telling myself it was just more thunder. Please, God, let it be thunder. It's thunder, right? But I knew. These were explosions, and they were getting louder. The sirens started going off. "Shit!" I thought. Before I really had time to come to terms with what was happening, something hit the hospital and shrapnel sprayed up the tin roof of our Quonset. "Oh no, no, no," I kept thinking. "No!" Please. Don't tell me I've gotten through these last few weeks only to die in a mortar attack the night before I'm supposed to leave.

Kay and the other nurses started grabbing guys from their beds and putting them underneath, like a two- or three-inch mattress would save their lives. "No!" I insisted, feeling guilty I was making one of them pause to have the discussion. I knew I was probably better on the ground than above it as in any other explosion, but a mattress wasn't going to give me much protection and wasn't worth the excruciating pain I would endure to be moved under it. "God has brought me through this much," I thought, "he isn't going to let me die now."

Kay didn't fight me. Decades after the war she did remember that one guy wouldn't go under his bed. "Don't you remember, Kay?" I told her. "That was me."

We both remember what happened next. She took off her flak jacket and laid it across my chest.

I was still taking in that particular act of kindness when a sergeant came running into the barracks. He bolted into the intensive-care ward and instead of helping the nurses he got scared and hid under a table. I am uncharacteristically sympathetic where he is concerned. You just don't know how you are going to react until you're in the situation.

The rounds continued for twenty minutes. That is to say, forever. I mean, it was just this little tin building and had a round penetrated the roof—God only knows why none of them ever did—it would have obliterated everyone inside.

The next time one hit the roof I thought, oh my God, how many times can they miss? It was almost like the night Godbout died. We're under fire, they have their shit together, it's only a matter of time.

I was absolutely sure God would pull me through this, and absolutely sure I was going to die. It didn't make sense. Nothing made sense.

I'm guessing this was just your garden-variety carpet mortar. The VC were always pounding, pounding, pounding away at our base camp, but sometimes they'd target our fuel or ammo dumps. You hit an ammo dump with mortar like that—now that's an explosion.

The hospital was just another target to the enemy, of course. It didn't matter if you were lying in a hospital bed, you were the enemy and would only be spared fire if you were already dead. It was the same in the field. In fact someone told me there were medics who didn't even want guys to holler "Medic!" because Charlie would make a point of shooting at them, too.

Here I go again, I kept thinking. Twenty minutes of terror and plenty of time to think about how this really could be the end of me. I couldn't shake the memory of one group of guys at base camp over Christmas. They were having a party in their hooch the night before they were to leave for home and there was a mortar attack similar to the one we were having now. They should have run out to their bunkers, but apparently they thought, oh to hell with it, Charlie isn't going to get me this late in my tour. A round came right into the hooch and killed every one of them.

I never got that sure of anything in Vietnam. I would have run for the bunker. People die when they're getting mortared. The shells that are dropping don't have happy bulletins on them.

They're trying to kill you. So it's your last day in country. So much the better.

Ostroot wrote in one letter to my folks that things were picking up because of the Tet Offensive. The Tet Offensive was a series of attacks by the North Vietnamese on more than a hundred urban targets, and the casualties were devastating. Doctors referred to wounded men coming into the Evac stacked like cordwood, it was that hard to keep up with it all.

The pace had picked up in hell, and whether I'd make it out after all was anyone's guess. Particularly tonight. The explosions just kept coming. You couldn't hear yourself think and it was almost like you were watching the nurses from a distance, trying to organize the chaos. I'd look down the ward at all these empty beds, now that their occupants were on the floor, and it was eerie. Once in a while I'd wonder if I was dreaming, or if I had died after all. Then more pain would shoot through my leg and I knew I was alive.

Am I dreaming this now, too? I wondered. Because it almost seemed like the explosions were getting further apart. Yes. They were. They're dwindling. Oh God, we are going to get through this. It's over. Is it over? Yes! It's over. It was like coming off the ice blankets again. The nurses started coming around, moving guys back onto their beds. Their agonized chorus of whimpers and groans was the sweetest sound in the world to me, because it meant we were still alive and I was going to get out of there.

About nine, ten o'clock the next morning they brought a stretcher over to my bed. "You're going home," someone said.

I'm going home.

I'm going home!

Bruce Ashworth was at the door when they carried me out of the building. "I would never have believed this day would happen, Jon," he admitted. "I must be the luckiest man alive," I thought. I was too weak to say it, though. I just kind of waved at him as they wheeled me toward the transport plane. I was still hurting so much.

They put my file on top of my stretcher. It must have been twelve inches thick with paper. All my orders, all my medical records, everything. That's the last I ever saw of it, too, because by the time I got to Japan no one could find it. Somehow it had gotten lost, and there wasn't much of a record of me even being in the war. Ironic, considering the shape I was in.

My first stop was to be a hospital in Saigon. I was being taken there on a C-130—a big cargo plane—with green and brown camouflage. It was waiting for me on a landing strip near the 12th Evac. We were only twenty-five miles from Saigon, so it wasn't going to be a long flight, but flying was the safest way out of there. I couldn't take this much longer, it hurt so much to be moved. It wouldn't have mattered how smooth the flight was. This was killing me.

We hadn't been in the air for even five minutes, I'm guessing, when the pilot came on and told us we wouldn't be landing in Saigon as planned. It's being overrun, he said. You're kidding, I thought. Right away I was so glad we hadn't left even an hour earlier.

The pilot was diverted to the 12th United States Air Force Hospital in Cam Ranh Bay, where I learned just how close I came to not making it out of Vietnam alive after all. The VC had made a major run at Saigon and were trying to take it out. I found out much later that my outfit was called in to help defend it and we lost a number of men. Charlie literally got into the hospital, from what I was told, and killed guys right in their beds. They shot at point-blank range—nurses, doctors, everyone. No one was spared. They weren't successful at taking over the city, but they hurt us bad. If my plane had left two hours earlier, I could easily have been one of the casualties.

That call was so close my hometown newspaper, the *Fertile Journal*, ran a story after my parents got a wire or letter or something, saying that I'd been handed an M-16 in my Saigon hospital bed and told to defend myself. That was false, just totally false. I mean, a couple of hours earlier and I guess that would have been the case. But luckily for me, it wasn't. I took more than a moment to think about those who hadn't been so lucky.

Cam Ranh Bay wasn't a forty-bed Quonset hut like I was used to. It was just one big ward with wall-to-wall beds. They got me settled into mine and I looked over at the guy in the next bed. He was a full-bird colonel if I remember him right, an older guy. Well, at least fifty—that was old to me back then. He'd lost his leg after being shot down in a helicopter and he leaned over to say something to me. I can't remember what it was, but I started to cry.

I hadn't cried the entire time I'd been in the field, and I hadn't cried for twenty-three days at the 12th Evac. Now I couldn't stop crying. I don't think it was so much what he said as the relief. Cam Ranh Bay was about as secure as it got in Vietnam, and I was starting to think I would make it home for sure. All the stress from just the last couple of days had been building up inside, not to mention the constant stress from the three months before, and I was a fountain of grief.

I thought I'd be on a plane to Japan the next day, but I probably should have known better. No, they told me, I wouldn't be leaving tomorrow or even the next day. There was nothing to do but lie there. No TV, nothing. So when I finally got my orders for Japan, I thought, "At *last*."

The TWA I would be flying on had seats like any other plane, until you got about halfway back. The back half of it had racks for stretchers, three tiers on each. They were almost like gun racks. There was room for at least fifteen, maybe eighteen or more stretchers. The tail section of the plane folded down so they could carry the stretchers in. We didn't board the front of the plane the way the other passengers did. There was a doctor on the flight and at least three nurses, and all of them were scurrying around, making sure we were ready for takeoff.

It hurt to fly. Oh, it hurt. Before we left I refused to get a shot of morphine or whatever they were offering. They didn't insist, but warned me that with all the bouncing around the pain pills I'd been taking probably wouldn't help much. By now I was starting to be afraid of getting hooked on painkillers, and took pride in turning them down whenever I could. I wanted to be the tough guy.

Takeoff wasn't that bad, actually. But I was on the second tier of this rack, and there was a guy above me and a guy below. The guy above me had been hit in the face, and that face was all ripped up. He was blind in both eyes. Pus was draining out of them and he was screaming. "I need some Kleenex! Give me some Kleenex! I have to wipe my eyes! Bring me some Kleenex!" He was wild, thrashing around on this rack and driving the rest of us absolutely freaking crazy—so much so *I* started hollering for the nurse. "You have to do something! You have to get me off of this thing! Or get him off of it. Something. He's killing us!"

The nurse told me they'd give him a hypo and he'd go to sleep. That's what they did, and that was the end of any problems with him. I can still feel how my body settled down once they gave him a shot. It just put him right to sleep. "Thank God," I said. "I couldn't have taken that much longer."

"Now I have something for you," one of the nurses told me after what didn't seem like very long at all. Apparently the flight wasn't a long one because she was already worried about how I would bear the pain of landing. "The doctors have ordered this shot for you," she said, "and this time you don't have a choice." She hit me with it almost before she finished her sentence and I was asleep right away.

When I woke up, everyone was gone. The last bus was pulling away from the tail end of the plane. I mean, the doctor and nurses were there, but I had been left behind. "What about me?" I hollered. "That bus is leaving! It's the last bus!"

"No, Jon," one nurse told me. "They're not going to put you on a bus."

"What *are* they going to do with me?"

"The doctor has ordered a helicopter for you."

"You're kidding."

"No," she said. "You've been through enough already. They're not going to let you jiggle around on a bus."

Wow. I'm a pretty lucky dude, I thought. No arm, no leg, no plans for the future, but no matter. They were treating me like royalty and I loved it. It was early February by now, and I saw three inches of snow on the ground. It felt like home. A helicopter and snow! I swore I could see around the world to Minnesota. It felt great.

Until I got into the hospital in Japan. Because the first thing the man at the end of my stretcher wanted to know was the last time I'd had a bowel movement.

"I don't remember."

"You don't remember what?"

"I don't think I've had a bowel movement since I was wounded."

"Oh God," he said. He took a gloved finger, stuck it up my ass, and started digging it out of me. You want to talk pain. "No!" I screamed. "I can't handle this! My leg's killing me and now *this*? You have to get me something. You have to!" He fetched a hypo of morphine and went back to work tearing my insides out. When he finished he held up the steel pail to show me it was half full of crap.

"You *have* to feel better," the guy said.

"I'm so worn out I don't know what I feel," I fired back.

Granted he was just doing his job, but I wasn't in the mood to thank him for the indignity.

I wondered if the nurses back at the 12th Evac had ever had someone there as long as I'd been. Most guys they just stabilized and shipped out. They never had to worry about bowel movements. I wonder if they just didn't totally forget about me that way. I've been in touch with some of them by now, but honestly this is the last subject you'd broach.

I was in what they called a total infection ward in Japan. You had to wear a cap, gown, and gloves to even be in there. When it was time to rest up after having all the crap dug out of me, I got into bed and looked up at the TV. Being here was a big deal because there were TV sets everywhere, hanging from the ceiling. I hadn't even seen a TV in all the time I was in Vietnam. The Bee Gees were singing their song "Massachusetts," and it really got to me. Still does. Even today when I hear that song I'm right back in the hospital in Japan.

It was way past time to change the casts on my arm and leg and clean up all the wire stitches underneath, so they soon took me in for the first of many surgeries. It was always something, though I've long since forgotten the reason for most of them.

When I left Vietnam I got a paycheck for $238, but I had no place to put it. I had no pockets, no wallet, nothing. Kay put the money in a white envelope and taped it to the cast on my arm. By the time I was supposed to go in for the first surgery I had kind of forgotten about it, and when I got out of surgery it was gone. A few minutes later some guy walked up and handed it to me, but he was pissed. "What the hell are you doing, having your money taped to your cast?" he wondered. "Where the hell else was I going to put it?" I snapped.

I was supposed to be in Japan for thirty days, which depressed me, but I wasn't strong enough to make the trip back to the States. To give you an idea of how weak I was, I didn't have the strength to move the dial on my Zippo lighter. I hadn't had a cigarette in those twenty-three days at the hospital in Cu Chi and should have taken the opportunity to quit smoking, period. But everybody else in my ward was smoking now, and I wanted to. A Red Cross lady stopped by my bed and asked if I needed anything. She offered to write letters for me, whatever. "I really need a cigarette lighter," I admitted. "I can't spin the dial on this one." She thought I was kidding, but after I tried to spin it right in front of her, she agreed. I told her I thought one of the butane lighters would work better, so she went uptown and got me a fliptop lighter.

I couldn't get that one to work either, so she put a rubber band on it to tighten it up. That helped. It took me forever to light it the first time, but I worked on it all afternoon and it finally happened. I pushed down and thought, "Damn. I got it lit!" That was such a big deal. But I couldn't do it twice in a row. I had the strength to do it once, but not twice.

The nurses would light our cigarettes, but I couldn't bring myself to ask them. If guys were at my bed, fine, I'd have them do it, but I thought it was rude to ask a nurse to light my cigarette.

About two o'clock every morning, it seemed, I woke up craving a cigarette.

The first night with my butane lighter I woke up and thought, okay, here goes. I'm going to have myself a cigarette. I pushed down on it and—yes! I got her lit! I was so excited. Excitement quickly gave way to despair, however, when I realized what an idiot I'd been. "Shit!" I thought. "I don't have a cigarette in my mouth!" I mean, how was I going to do this? I have a flame, but I don't have a cigarette. I'm going to have to drop the lighter, put a cigarette in my mouth, and then try to light it. I couldn't do it though. I couldn't get the lighter going again. That's frustration.

The simplest things, like lighting my own cigarette, were not so simple anymore. Not with one hand.

I waited until morning for my cigarette.

I didn't feel put upon, though, not after what I'd been through. So I couldn't have a cigarette whenever I wanted? So what? I was beginning to realize there were plenty of guys who'd given a lot more for their country than I had. Whining is unbecoming.

The guy on the other side of my bed reminded me. He had lost his leg defending Khe Sanh and was always whining to the nurses that he needed more morphine. I listened to him for most of an entire day before I finally leaned over to him and asked him what the deal was. "I'm a runner," he said, "and I'm never going to be able to run again." I looked at him. "Crap," I said. "You're going to be able to walk without a limp!" His leg had been amputated quite a bit below the knee. "I don't know about running in marathons, but you're in pretty good shape from what I can tell."

He was unmoved by my little speech and kept pestering the nurses for something to kill the pain. How much pain can there be in a leg that isn't there anymore? I thought, growing increasingly frustrated by him. One afternoon I was trying to concentrate on a letter I was writing—I'd had someone tape a pencil to my cast so I could work on it—and he just wouldn't let up. So finally I said, "I have an idea. You take your cigarettes and go across the ward and talk to Tom Bailey." Tom was the guy who had been in the bed next to me at the 12th Evac for a while. "If you come back and you feel the same way," I continued, "by God, I'll sit here and holler with you. We'll get you more dope than you can handle."

He took his cigarettes and damned if he wasn't gone for more than an hour. I was almost finished with my letter when he got back. Out of the corner of my eye I could see him get out of his wheelchair and slither back into his bed. He was just lying there, not saying a word. Finally after a minute or two he kind of turned his head to me and said, "Jon, I'm sorry." And then, "You know that guy, don't you?" And I said, "Yeah." And he said, "My God, all he lost and he's so happy! The broadest smile I've ever seen. How can that be? I look at you, and I'm twice as well off as you. You have two limbs gone, I only have one. He has three limbs gone, so you're better off than him." He paused. "What do you think keeps him going?" he asked.

"I don't know," I said. "But sometimes it takes a guy like that to remind the rest of us what we have."

Every time I started wondering what the hell I was going to do with myself, I thought about Tom—and I stopped worrying. It really was that simple. I knew I couldn't go back to the construction work I had been doing in California with my uncle before I went off to war. You can't be walking a Glu-Lam beam sixty-five feet in the air with one leg and one arm. It just isn't going to happen. So I knew my career as a journeyman carpenter was over. I figured I'd have to go to college, something that never occurred to me before the army. I had had teachers who said I didn't have the brains to go to college. Now that I didn't have the body to do anything else, I decided, whatever brains I did have were going to have to pull more weight.

CHAPTER 5

Moving On

I've never had nightmares about Vietnam.

Hard to believe, isn't it?

I started to get some real sleep in Japan. I was no longer worried about dying, and while my first night on ambush patrol basically ruined my chance of a normal night's sleep *ever*, I was getting more of it here. I wrote lots of letters, and I looked forward to going home.

Home was to be the Walter Reed Army Medical Center in Washington, D.C. They had a big amputee center there. My sister called Odin Langen's office—he was the congressman from my home district—and got the orders changed within hours. I couldn't believe how quickly they responded to her request. I was now assigned to Letterman General Hospital in San Francisco, where I'd be close to my uncle, a bunch of cousins, and Darlene.

It was toward the end of February when I found out I was leaving for California. You cannot imagine how light that felt. In the last month I had been starting to get around better and better. My leg still hurt, but not nearly as much. I hadn't put any weight on it and didn't know if I'd be able to stand up, but I was optimistic about coming home and actually recovering. The doctors told me

I'd wear prosthetics and be fine, but you never really knew until you start using them. I didn't worry about it, though. I was too excited about going home.

I landed at Travis Air Force Base on the second of March, a day earlier than expected. My parents were coming out the day they thought I was going to arrive, March 3. People in my hometown had raised money to pay for their trip. Neither one of them had ever been on an airplane before.

Travis is fifty miles northeast of San Francisco. I took the bus from there to Letterman because my leg was better by then. When I first got into my bunk at the hospital a Red Cross lady came by and told me I was entitled to a free phone call home and any meal I wanted. "If you want a T-bone steak, that's fine," she said. "Whatever you want. You get one meal any way you like." They wheeled a telephone on a little cart over to my bed. My parents were on their way to California. My sister Karen answered the phone and I heard could hear the song "Tunesmith" by Johnny Rivers playing in the background. Before I left for Vietnam I used to play that over and over, and now Karen told me they'd played it so much while I was gone the record was almost worn out. I talked to her and my other sister, Lana, for at least an hour and a half.

I know it was that long because the Red Cross lady was at my bed again. "I should have told you that the phone call was only supposed to be a half hour." She smiled, knowing I'd taken closer to two hours. "That's okay," she said, still smiling.

I ordered my meal. A cheeseburger with fries and a chocolate malt. I remembered that steak was one of the options, but I was like a lot of guys in Vietnam—we just craved a plain old hamburger.

I had arrived about noon, and by late afternoon I had company. I was lying in my bed in the ward, and saw Darlene first. My uncle and cousins were with her, but I didn't even see them. I don't remember what Darlene was wearing but I can still see her face. She looked good. Oh man, I thought, it's all been worth it. It's all been worth it.

Right away I braced myself for her reaction. Until now my amputations were only a theory. Now she was seeing them for herself. Then what? Would she still love me?

She kind of hung back while everyone said hello, which scared me. "Come over here and give me a hug," I suggested. So she did. We hugged, we kissed, we took each other in. We just looked into each other's eyes and knew. Nothing had changed. We were in love, we were still the same people, that was all there was to it. She was my girl.

To this day people cannot understand how Darlene knew as a junior in high school that she was ready to get married at all, let alone marry someone facing the physical challenges I faced. She says she can understand the perception that she was too young to get married, though no one could have told her so at the time. What she doesn't understand, and in fact can get very put off by, is how anyone could think her feelings toward me would change just because of the amputations. She's actually had people come up to her after one of my speeches and say, "*Thank you* for staying with him." That gets under her skin. It never entered her mind, she says, to feel differently toward me, and she can't help wondering about those who do change when something like this happens. She wonders if they were ever in love to begin with.

Darlene and the rest stayed for a couple of hours that first day and came back at least a few times a week from that point on. She kept my spirits up. Nothing a doctor might order could compare.

My folks arrived the second day. There was a big, older nurse—a really tough old bird, if you'll forgive me—who got to my mom before she got to me. "Now when you see him for the first time," she warned, "don't cry, because that's not going to help him." She and my dad approached my bed and of course all three of us started bawling immediately, and nobody stopped for the longest time. I didn't find out until a few years ago what that nurse had said, and I'm still trying to figure out what the hell she could have been thinking.

My parents stayed for a week. My uncle brought them to the hospital every day—I think he took a week off work. His favorite food was homemade donuts, so my mom made those in the morning. The three of them came over in the afternoon, spent two or three hours with me, and then went back to my uncle's place.

My parents got to know a lot of the other guys. Dad, especially, loved joking around with them and talked about a few for years after that. He had one heck of a time on those visits.

Most of what I remember from my first few weeks at Letterman was another barrage of surgeries. In and out, in and out again. It was always something.

There were probably forty guys in the room I was in. Letterman was a big hospital and only blocks from Haight-Ashbury, home of hippies and war protesters. I couldn't see them from my window, but I will never forget one of them paying us a visit. He was in this little coffee shop just down the hall from my ward. I happened to be in there with another amputee. We were in our wheelchairs when he strolled in, wearing a dirty Class A army jacket and looking defiant. Just the fact he was so dirty, I knew he was making a statement. He had long hair and a beard and was a really greasy, grubby-looking guy—every bit what you imagine when you think of Haight-Ashbury, at least in those days.

I got so damn mad at the sight of him that I told my buddy

I was going to wheel over there and whack him one with my cane. I knew it was his right to protest the war, but to do it right in front of us! Someone with balls that big should be taken out, and I was more than happy to oblige.

I went after him in my wheelchair with my cane poised— like I could do a lot of damage at my then-weight of ninety-eight pounds. "You think I'm a weakling?" I said with my eyes. "Let me show you how much my rage will compensate for that." I was still wheeling toward him when out of nowhere an MP showed up and stopped me. "I'll take care of this," he said, and grabbed the guy. I don't know who the MP thought was trying to make a bigger statement, the hippie or me. He knew what I was thinking, put it that way. What was one more scar? It didn't matter. I wanted to pound this guy's head with my wooden cane.

As the MP escorted him out of the building I heard part of the butt chewing: "You know," he said, "I have half a mind to take you down to the ward where this soldier came from and set you in the doorway. We'll see what's left of you when you come out the other end." You could tell he wasn't kidding. And that was it. The guy left, and I don't remember seeing anyone like that in the hospital again.

It was strange to watch news of the war on TV. For one thing, Vietnam was really the first time things unfolded right in your living room—or in my case, in your hospital ward. You couldn't get away from it. There were reports on every channel, on the front page of every newspaper, and in the headlines of almost every radio newscast. That's what I remember anyway. So many Americans were killed today, they'd say, so many Vietnamese. Yeah, right. I thought back to the cemetery and knew whoever was reporting was probably full of more shit than I had been.

I read the papers, but I had no idea what was going on with my outfit. That was Vietnam. We totally lost touch with each other once we left. No one I know ever got a list, for example, with the full names and addresses of the men in their outfit. That was just the way it was. For a long time I wondered if it was a way of protecting us from each other. Maybe there was a hope that collectively we could all just forget enough of the details to ease back into a normal life somehow. As if that were possible.

I think I was different from a lot of veterans in that I don't feel that the war changed me. A lot of soldiers came back from Vietnam depressed and forever down on life, but I came out of it almost better for the experience. I appreciate everything so much more. I lost two limbs, but I don't really think about them. I think about the two limbs I *have*.

It's not that I didn't see horrible things. I did. I just didn't dwell on them. I chose to think about the good things I saw. Like Nurse Kay taking off her flak jacket and laying it across my chest during a mortar attack.

I knew I could never forget the many people who saved my life. I knew I could never protest the war because to me that would be like saying my friends had died in vain. I don't think I have a right to say that. Plus, I really did believe in what we were doing over there. You can talk about poverty in America, but from what I saw it just didn't compare to what I saw in Vietnam.

My two stumps weren't sutured shut, which was part of the reason I had to be hospitalized so long. I had to wait for them to heal from the inside out. They weren't closed with stitches because from what they told me, there was less chance of an infection that way. I have four inches of leg and four inches of arm on my left side, and the stumps were packed in gauze soaked in a solution to keep everything clean. Gradually they required less gauze and pretty soon the skin just kind of grew back.

It took a long time. Your stump has to be totally healed

before you can be fitted into a prosthetic. I was still waiting for mine to heal when I first got to Letterman.

There were plenty of other problems to distract me from not being able to learn to walk yet. There was the not-so-small matter of my penis, which still had a chunk of shrapnel inside and may have been the reason I still couldn't urinate on my own. When that mine went off, nothing escaped the blast—and I mean nothing. In fact that's what Bruce Ashworth told me he remembers the most. "Oh my God," he said, after looking at some pictures. "I forgot how bad you took it in the nuts." He told me he can't imagine how much that hurt. I don't remember, believe it or not, because every-thing else hurt more. But think about it. I was slammed against this iron. You think it hurts to get hit in that area with a baseball? Make it a bowling ball, fired out of a cannon. I felt like I was in the horror-movie version of *America's Funniest Home Videos*.

Especially when the doctor in San Francisco told me how he proposed getting at the shrapnel, which he discovered after more X-rays. "I'm going to peel that thing like a banana." I looked at him. "That's the easiest way for me to explain it," he said. "You've peeled a banana before, haven't you?" Oh God, I thought, will you *stop*? I couldn't even imagine how much that would hurt, but was fairly sure they'd put me to sleep—and they did.

When I came out of this particular surgery on about the first day of spring, 1968, there was a big wire cage resting over the middle of my body. A sheet covered that, so it was like there was a tent protecting my penis. Not so much from the surgery—well, okay, that too—but from onlookers. Because it was *huge*. All those bandages! A sight to behold. There was a first sergeant in the bed next to me, and after I came to he leaned over and said, "My God, what did they do to you this time?"

"I had some shrapnel taken out of my penis."

"Can I look?"

I guess so.

He pulled the sheet up and said, "Damn. I wonder if *I* could get one of those." And we all had a good laugh, especially when the nurse told me why it was packed in ice: "If you get an erection, you'll ruin everything. All the stitches will come out and we'll have to start over."

This was no laughing matter. Once when Darlene was visiting, just standing by my bed and talking to me, the ice started melting. "Dar!" I screamed. "Get out of here!"

"What?" she asked. "What's going on?" She wasn't so much hurt as confused.

"I'll explain later. Just get the hell out of here! *Please!*"

They packed that sucker with more ice, and I breathed the latest sigh of relief.

I scratched little pieces of shrapnel out of my head for almost two years after the war, too. The nurses warned me about this. Tiny little fragments of metal would just continue to work their way out of my body for years. We hoped.

I got to be good friends with the first sergeant bunking next to me. Each outfit had one. We called them "Top."

This Top and I were good friends, and he looked out for me. The little cart with the pay phone had wheels made of steel, and you could hear it coming. It was usually right in the middle of the ward, or next to whomever had used it last. It rang a lot, but no one jumped up to answer it—except me. I'd hop into my wheelchair to get it, even though most of the time the call wasn't for me. I always hoped it would be Darlene, or Mom or Dad, and sometimes it was, but most of the time it was for somebody else. It wasn't long before I'd answered the phone one too many times to suit Top. The next time it rang he jumped out of his bed and said, "Many of you are way better off than Jon. You have both legs and one good arm. If I have to see him jump into his wheelchair one more time to answer that damn phone there's going to be hell to pay." The next time it rang guys tripped over each other to get it. "I guess we solved that problem," Top said, winking at me.

There were many days when Top turned to me and said, "Let's go for a ride, Jon." He helped me into my wheelchair and pushed me around the hospital grounds. We enjoyed each other's company and he kept my spirits up, too.

I was still in and out of surgery all the time. They operated on my eye to remove a growth—something I can't spell or pronounce. Then I had a stone removed from my bladder. You get the idea.

Eventually the stumps healed and I was fitted for a prosthetic arm and leg. I got my arm first. The arm I have today is basically the same as the one I had back then. It's attached with what they call a figure-eight strap. When I lean forward the hook opens and I can grasp whatever it is. I lean back and the hook closes. I played a lot of checkers in the hospital. That was my physical therapy, learning to pick up big wooden checkers.

I've always felt blessed it was my left arm I lost because I'm right-handed. I only have three good fingers on my right hand, but I can outtype my son-in-law on the computer.

I took my first steps in May 1968. For all the drama that led up to this milestone, the moment wasn't set to music or anything—though the very first step was met with applause. I just did what I had to do, hundreds of hours of physical therapy. A lot of hard work, some of it very boring. But I got better.

Learning to walk again was just a metaphor, of course, for the freshness I felt about my life. The future held only promise. Everything was ahead of me and I looked forward to all of it.

Part of the reason I felt so at peace was the security of the hospital. Surrounded by amputees, there wasn't the isolation that would settle in once I got home. I knew what was expected of me in the hospital. I tried not to worry about the abyss that awaited me once I was released, though I did take an accounting class when I was there. I don't know if I even earned credit for it, but it bolstered my confidence and gave me something to do.

For entertainment we did wheelies in the hallway. Picture it—three or four of us at a time raising as much hell as it's possible to raise in wheelchairs. The nurses didn't like it because we could fall over backward and get hurt even more, though no one ever did, not that I saw anyway. "Hey!" they'd holler. "You're not supposed to be doing that!" And we'd stop until they were almost out of sight, then start in again. It struck me, how much fun we were having. At the time I don't think I realized how important it was to be with other amputees. I'm sure it helped to look in any direction and find someone worse off than you were. And I'm sure it was what the higher-ups had in mind when they sent us all to the same place.

We had a lot of visits from celebrities while I was at Letterman. I have a photo of me with Barbara McNair and one with Della Reese. An actor from a TV show called *The Rat Patrol* came up to my bed, but I didn't recognize him. "You don't know who I am, do you?" I think he said. His show was only on for a couple of years. I also got to meet Willard Waterman, whom I'd listened to on the radio as a kid. He played *The Great Gildersleeve* and I recognized his voice right away. He was a big guy, six foot five. But that radio voice! It was fun to meet him.

I bought a car while I was still in the hospital. It was a sharp car—not my dream car, mind you, that was a GTO—but a '60 Chevy two-door hardtop Impala with chrome reversed rims. I just needed something to get around in once I found out I was going to get weekend passes. That was really exciting, because Darlene only lived a block from my uncle. If I went to my uncle's for the weekend, I could see her all the time. I drove to my uncle's on Friday night and didn't have to go back to the hospital until Sunday night.

Since I had my right arm and I'm right-handed, I could drive with an automatic transmission. Any kind of car trouble would mean real trouble, though, even—or maybe especially—a flat tire. But I could get myself out to the car in my wheelchair, throw the wheelchair in the trunk, and then hop around and get in the car and drive.

I'll never forget being taken for a driver's license test with two other amputees. There was a crowd of people there and I could hear a couple of elderly women say, "I hope they don't give those men a license!" I inspired a fair amount of skepticism when I bought the car, for that matter. My uncle took me to the dealership, where it seemed like everyone was consumed by how the hell someone with one arm and one leg thought he was going to drive.

My license said I was not allowed to drive a stick transmission—it still does—but I didn't need any special equipment in my car. That was a great feeling. Six hundred bucks for independence. I was more excited to be driving than I had been at sixteen.

Back in the hospital, it became more of a game to see how much we could get by with. John Petty was in the bed next to me for a while; he had lost both his arms while riding in a lowboy truck with a bulldozer on the back. They were turning a corner and Petty saw the back wheels of this trailer come off. "God!" he said, knowing something really bad was about to happen. He was thrown out of the semi-truck and had his arms extended over his head when the blade of the bulldozer came down and sheared off both his arms. He told me he'd crawled into the bushes and had wanted to die. He had hoped he'd bleed to death because he couldn't imagine life without arms.

That changed once he got to Letterman. It may be hard to believe, but we had fun. Petty made a habit of hanging from those triangle trapeze bars they had above some of our beds. He stuck both his legs through it and swung from it. The nurses didn't seem to mind. Petty had blonde, curly hair and was really good-looking. We called him the nurse's pet. He was definitely a ladykiller, even with no arms. And every night, I swear, three or four nurses would come in and kiss him goodnight. I kid you not.

The rest of us were not treated as kindly by the nurses—or the doctors, for that matter. I don't know if my doctor was having a bad day or what, but there was one time he decided we'd done too many wheelies and shouldn't get weekend passes. I got that word on a Friday, after I knew my uncle was already on his way. "I can't leave," I told him when he arrived. "We got caught doing wheelies and that's our punishment."

My uncle Randy, who has since died of cancer, was six foot three and meaner than hell back then, your basic barroom brawler. "What's your doctor's name?" he demanded. "I'm going to find that SOB. Just get your stuff together. I'll be back, and you're leaving."

I believed him. I got my shit together and was ready when Randy returned. We left. No one gave us any trouble.

I wasn't the only guy with a weekend pass. Most people got them eventually. Petty would go into downtown San Francisco to party and come back with as much money as he left with. People wouldn't take the money out of his shirt pocket like he told them to, and it wasn't like he could hand it to them. He didn't drink a lot of beer, but he had to do it through a straw, so he got drunk faster.

I felt bad for him though. He couldn't wipe his own ass before he got his hooks, although come to think of it, I don't know how he did it after either. But before then he had to have the nurses do it and he hated it—just hated it. One day he said, "Jon, would you ever consider doing that for me? It's so humiliating to have the nurses do it." I told him sure. I'd wheel into the bathroom with him. He'd go, I'd wipe, and I never thought anything of it.

I did for Petty, and my uncle did for me. Sometimes Randy carried me up an entire flight of stairs into someone's house or wherever it was. Once I got my leg he'd put Johnny Horton's song on, "Johnny Reb," and want to see me walking every time he played it, which was a lot.

> You fought for your folks but you didn't die in vain.
> Even though you lost, they speak highly of your name.
> 'Cause you fought all the way, Johnny Reb, Johnny Reb.
> You fought all the way, Johnny Reb.

"If you fall, I'll pick you up," he said. "But you're going to learn to walk." So that's what I did. I learned to walk on the weekends. My right leg hurt so much, and my new, artificial left leg weighed thirty pounds back in those days. So getting around was quite a feat. I didn't complain, though. I was so happy to be getting around on my own power.

In June I got a week's pass and flew home to Minnesota. I was supposed to be in coach for the flight to Minneapolis, but the stewardesses moved me up to first class, which I'd never been in before. I had my Class A army jacket on because otherwise I wouldn't be able to fly military standby and get the military rate. I was supposed to wear my stripe and my Purple Heart, too, but I didn't. I just didn't want to. It wasn't just how the general public seemed to feel about the war. It was also this motto we had, that you take a Purple Heart to the coffee shop and you still had to pay fifteen cents for a cup of coffee. In fact when I got home I cut the ribbon off of it and was going to have it made into a keychain, but never got around to it. The only reason I ever took it out was to show to kids when I spoke at schools.

I was enjoying my first-class digs when a stewardess asked if I wanted anything to drink. I hadn't been drinking much since the war, believe it or not. I hadn't had more than a few beers with my uncle once in a while. "No, thank you," I said. "I want to be able to walk off this plane." That was a big deal. To walk! I wanted my family to see me walk off the plane.

"Well," the stewardess said, "how about a little champagne? That'll kind of take the edge off."

That it would.

"Maybe one glass wouldn't hurt," I told her.

"It has to be tough," she told me, "going home for the first time."

One glass led to a second, and then a third. I don't know how many I eventually drank, but it was a pile. I had one hell of a time talking to those stewardesses. I never had to ask for more champagne. My glass was always full.

Soon I found out what those little brown puke bags were for. There would be no walking off this plane. I'd like to report how good Minnesota looked to me when we landed, but I was too hammered to know—though in my defense it was also dark outside. A couple of my sisters and their husbands picked me up, but nobody thought anything of my little champagne supper. They were just glad to see me.

I didn't do much the week I was home. For one thing it was still really difficult to get around. I just stayed at the house and hung out with the friends who came to visit, off and on, all week. My mom waited on me, I remember that. I never had to ask for anything. Everyone seemed so glad to have me home.

Once I returned to Letterman after that week it was just a matter of getting strong enough to go home for good. The last thing I remember happening before then was going into a room with one of the doctors and lying on a table for at least an hour

while he did range-of-motion tests. He measured how much movement I had in my right foot and ankle, he counted my stitches
and measured them, he measured how much movement I had in
my right arm and hand, and then how much movement in my fingers. He went over every square inch of me, poking, prodding,
making notes. Finally he put the clipboard down.

"You're 165 percent disabled," he announced.

What?

"How in the hell can I be more than 100 percent disabled?"
I asked.

He said the magnitude of my injuries pushed me into the
statutory awards. You can be anywhere from 0 to 100 percent disabled, and then on up. I was in the "on up" category, meaning
there were statutory awards for injuries from A through O, with
O being the most severe. I was N. I was almost as bad off as they
had designations for, and that meant I'd get paid more.

I was discharged from the service on September 28, 1968.
At that point I no longer drew my regular army pay, my $228 a
month. That's what I'd been collecting the whole time I was in the
hospital. Instead I got a raise, to $336 a month. They adjust that
for inflation, and I don't pay taxes on it. It's tax-free, forever.
That's my compensation for being a disabled veteran.

I was eager to get out of the hospital. There wasn't much
more they could do for me. I wanted to get back home to Minnesota. I knew I'd miss Darlene, but I kept telling her I'd be back.
She still had a year left in high school.

My twin sister, Cathy, flew out that August—I was released
from the hospital before my official discharge date from the service—and we took my car back to Fertile. I drove the entire way.
She says she'll never forget that. I wouldn't let her drive. We got
there in record time, too. I couldn't wait to get home.

Any apprehension I felt about returning to real life was

muted by the excitement I felt at not being hospital-bound. There was some apprehension, I admit. I still could only walk five or six steps before I started hurting so bad I had to sit down. I knew I'd need a wheelchair until that changed, which bothered me.

There aren't a lot of twenty-year-olds who know exactly what they're going to do with their lives, and I was typical that way—though I was also going to have more than my share of challenges. I tried not to worry about it too much.

The very first thing I remember about being home was the feeling I had as we pulled into our driveway. As a kid the neighbor boys and I were obsessed with basketball. We shot baskets all the time, even in the winter. It could be twenty below with a wicked wind, and we shoveled the snow out of the way and shot baskets. We kept the ball inside so it would bounce, but other than that we didn't let a little thing like a blizzard stand between us and more hoops.

Cathy and I drove into the driveway, and I parked right in front of the garage like I always had before. I looked up at the basketball hoop and my stomach sunk. "Well," I thought, "I guess I won't be shooting baskets anymore." The very next thing I saw was my bike, and I thought, "Well, I guess I won't be riding that anymore."

And so it went. The upbeat attitude I thought was my birthright drained out of me by the minute. Everywhere I turned, I saw reminders of what I couldn't do.

Why things like that hadn't dawned on me when I was home on a week's break, I don't know. Maybe because I wasn't there for good. Now I was, and it was depressing. Not only that, but my buddies—who of course came over right away—went out partying that night and didn't invite me.

I cried myself to sleep for the first time in my entire life.

The town of Fertile had a hero's welcome for me soon after I got home. It was a little reception at our church, Concordia Lutheran.

I hated it. I felt like I was on display. I've always been very shy, so shy that in elementary school my twin sister had to raise her hand to ask permission for *me* to use the bathroom. War hadn't helped where this was concerned. In fact it made it that much worse because I was so self-conscious about my hook. I didn't walk very well with that thirty-pound leg, and you can imagine the limp I had. But the hook! I felt like a freak.

It reminded me of a guy who was on the Fertile School Board for many years, Emil Peterson. He had lost his right arm in a corn picker, and as a kid I was afraid of him. He'd come walking down the sidewalk and I'd cross the street to avoid getting anywhere near that hook. It's funny thinking of that now, because up until he died a few years ago, when we bought gloves I'd give him my left glove and he'd give me his right one.

I don't think Emil even knew he was scaring me. I just stayed the heck out of his way. That's why today when I see kids staring at me, as they can't help doing, I make a point of talking to them and rolling up my sleeve and showing them everything so they're not afraid.

It wasn't just Emil I was afraid of when I was a kid. Think of it. The good guys in cartoons didn't have hooks. The scary ones had them, like Captain Hook.

It was such a sinking feeling, to realize I was the person I used to be afraid of.

I couldn't wait for the reception to be over. All these people dropping by for the sole purpose of saying hello and getting a good look at me.

One thing people often wonder is whether I have a second or two when I wake up before I remember that I'm wounded. I've never forgotten that for one moment. I'm hurting too much, even now. There's no relief from the pain. Usually it's my foot: to this day a doctor has to carve at a bone that grows right out of the bottom of it, but there's always something giving me fits.

There's no relief, not even in sleep.

There was some relief in the bars, though, and that's where I spent the next several months of my life. People ask, "What did you do when you got back from Vietnam?" And I tell them I was a drunk. No point in denying it. My dad had battled problems with alcohol his entire life, and now it was my turn. It wasn't like Dad was my drinking buddy, not at all. By now he'd had several heart attacks and wiled away the hours whittling wood in our living room. He made tables and stuff like that. Now that I was home we played checkers all day. Checkers and Yahtzee, all day—until it was time to meet up with my friends and head to the bars. Mom made Dad and me chicken noodle soup for lunch, which she served with Land O'Lakes cheese, and then we went back to our games.

My dad could never beat me at checkers. I'm serious. It was months before he won a single game and we both wanted to do something to mark the occasion. I took a pen to the checkerboard and wrote that Dad won this game, and I still have that board. It was a big deal.

Dad and I had always been close, and now we grew even closer. I'm the only son. Besides my twin sister, Cathy, I have two older sisters, Barbie and Karen, and a younger sister, Lana. Another sister, Peggy, died before I was born.

Ole Hovde was a railroad man. He ran the coal dock for Northern Pacific for many years, while my mom, Arleene, stayed home with us. Dad's book is the one I wish I could have written. He came to the United States in 1923 from Norway, where he was a ski-jumping champion. He wanted to make a living doing that, but this was long before you got prize money for excelling at the sport. It didn't take long before he realized he wasn't going to be able to support a family with a closetful of trophies.

You may have heard it said that perfect parenting is a contradiction in terms. You won't be ready to deal with challenges as an adult if you don't get any practice as a kid. I had my share of challenges growing up, but I don't know that I could have survived Vietnam otherwise. Most importantly, I knew I was loved, and that more than anything pulled me through.

Toward late afternoon my buddies from Vietnam, Roger Waddington and Keith Bolstad, would come over and we would go uptown to drink beer—after November 14, that is, when I turned twenty-one. That was our routine, and I don't remember missing very many days. My car payment was ninety bucks then, and I was living at home for free. Once in a while I'd buy T-bone steaks for a family dinner, but other than that I didn't have much in the way of expenses—and I spent most of my checks on beer.

My job was to heal up and recover, I thought, and my parents did nothing to dissuade me from the lifestyle I slipped into. No one knew any better at the time.

Every day we headed for the Fertile Municipal Liquor Store and bellied up. We'd get there at three, four o'clock in the afternoon and stay until closing. Many nights we'd then drive to Glyndon, Minnesota, for breakfast because that was the closest town with anything open at that hour. Glyndon is about fifty miles from Fertile.

I know what you're thinking. Drinking and driving. A lot. And it bothers me to think there will be young people reading this book, maybe getting the idea that I think that was okay. It wasn't okay. It was wrong. I'm not proud of it, but it's what I did.

We never got stopped and we never got in an accident. Not to excuse it, but just to explain how it was possible, I should add that I don't remember meeting a single car in all the trips we took. It was the absolute dead of night on the backroads of rural Minnesota. There just wasn't anybody around. Lucky for us—and for them.

One thing that stands out about this winter of disconnect was reading that Schlitz workers were going on strike. We all drank Schlitz. We liked Schlitz—it was our beer. One day we walked into the liquor store and Lloyd Olson, the bartender, told us that he was down to two and a half cases of it. We loved Lloyd: he was the stereotypical bartender in that everybody in town looked forward to his stories and the grin he wore as he delivered them.

Two and a half cases of Schlitz. Granted there were only three of us, but trust me, that wasn't going to last us until the end of the evening. We looked at each other and didn't say a word, but we knew what we had to do. We had to run him out of beer that night.

Hours went by. Rounds were pounded. Then it happened. I can still see Lloyd walking over with only two bottles. The third one he didn't have. "I'm sorry, boys," he said. "I'm out of Schlitz."

I couldn't believe it. He had no idea what was coming. That made it all the sweeter, of course, when the three of us stood up at the same time and said in unison, "Well, Lloyd, when you're out of Schlitz, you're out of beer."

Oh God, he roared. He just roared. He thought it was hilarious. *We* thought it was hilarious, but we were drunk. The fact he got such a kick out of that is a source of great pride to this very day.

I look back on those several months and find it interesting that we weren't thought of as the town drunks. At least I don't think that's the way people saw us. It was more the opposite, if anything. It's almost like people wondered how else we'd be coping.

I never got bored drinking, I'll tell you that. That was the thing. We liked it. We enjoyed it. There were always people to shoot the bull with and we were the masters at that. But I never really thought of us as sloppy-ass drunks. We were just friends who liked to party.

I remember a bar light on the west wall of the liquor store. I don't know how many nights I bought a pack of cigarettes only to smoke a few and swear the rest of them off. I'd throw the rest of the pack up there on that bar light. It's funny they didn't start a fire. I'd throw them away and say, I'm quitting this. Because you got more hung over from the cigarettes than the beer. "Jesus," I'd think. "Why do I keep doing this?" Sometimes I'd even throw cigarettes out the window of my car as I made the latest vow to quit. More than once I'd need one later and there wouldn't be anything open, so I'd go walking down the street trying to retrieve a few.

That was the one good thing about drinking. It strengthened my desire to quit smoking.

I obviously wasn't making much progress on my vow to make a difference with my life. But remember, that was my third vow. I was taking them in order, and the first order of business was to have the fastest car in Polk County.

I still had the Chevy Impala I bought in California when I drag raced Jerry Erickson one September night. He had a '63 Chevy with a 283 engine, and we went at each other on an eleven-mile stretch of winding road near Fertile. Earl Mosher was the sheriff back then and he started chasing us, trying to catch us on the curves. I thought we could outrun him, like we'd done other times, but we came over this little rise on the north end of town and there was a cop car sitting crosswise on the road, blocking us. Earl had called Wally Ellegaard, the city cop, on the radio and it was his car that stopped us.

That was my first speeding ticket after the war.

I don't remember the second ticket, other than that it was within two or three weeks of the first one. I do remember hearing they always come in threes.

By now I had traded in my Chevy for a '68 Dodge Charger with a 383 engine. I really wanted a 440, but it cost too much—though I got screwed so bad on the 383 I could have gotten the 440.

This was the age of the muscle car. It seemed like everyone who was coming home from Vietnam wanted one. Everyone, it seemed, had mufflers that didn't muffle a whole lot and hopped-up engines.

I put the Charger through the stupid-ass kid paces. We'd drive two hundred and fifty miles and never leave town, just back and forth on Main Street. That was during the week. On Saturdays we'd drive to Fargo and drag Broadway, which they don't allow anymore.

The fastest car usually led the pack, and the fastest car was almost always mine. Before Vietnam I had had a '57 Ford with a 312 four barrel. The speedometer would go to 130 and I'd bury that thing. A lot of times the cops wouldn't even go after me because they didn't want to drive as fast as they would have had to to catch me.

We raised hell with our cars, but we weren't destructive. Except for the time we laid rubber on the sidewalk all the way from the *Fertile Journal* to Eide's Store and almost clipped a light pole. That upset the business owners, but we never got caught. I suppose that will change with this book.

We raised hell, but we didn't get into fights. I came close one night when some guys stopped us as we drove around Crookston. One kid rolled down his window and hollered to me that it must be nice to have my mom buy me a car and all the tires I wanted. "My mom didn't buy this car," I hissed. One thing led to another. He called me a motherfucker, which I wasn't going to let pass. We pulled into an empty gas station in Crookston and I got out of the car. I stood against the Charger. I had to steady myself because if he swung at me and I fell I might not get up fast enough for it to matter. I wanted to take the first swing anyway.

Whether I'd use my hook, I didn't know. I knew I could do some damage with it, because about two weeks before a couple of guys had dared me to see what I could do to one of their cars, which was just a total piece of shit. I took a step back, did my windup, and went at the car door with everything I had. Of course the hook got stuck in the metal. What a sight we must have made, the three of us trying to free my arm from the side of that car.

"Just call me that name one more time," I dared the guy at the gas station. His eyes got wide as I continued. "I paid for this car with my limbs in Nam, and I'll tell you something. You may get the first swing, but I'll get the next one. When I hit you with this thing you're going to see stars for days." Just in case he didn't think I was serious, I locked my elbow. Otherwise the arm would just flop around. With it locked, you could kill someone. In fact a few years ago, a state hospital patient in Arizona was charged with assault with a deadly weapon after he hit a security officer with his prosthetic arm.

When I locked my arm, he turned sweet. "Oh, I don't want to be a prick or anything," he said. And that was that.

That was as close as I ever came to getting in a fight since Vietnam.

Fights just aren't my style and never have been, Vietnam vet or no. Even in boot camp I was pretty genteel.

I did get into one fight during jungle training in Georgia. We were running out of the barracks in the pouring rain to get into formation. Some guy, for whatever reason, tripped me and I fell in the mud. We had to have spit-shined boots and everything before we could fall into formation, and I was so mad at the guy I started pounding on him when I got up. I was on top of him when the drill sergeant appeared. "Do you know what you get for this?"

he asked. I should get a weekend pass, I thought to myself, because this guy's an asshole.

I didn't get a weekend pass. I got KP duty for three days. The other guy didn't get anything.

I was pissed. KP duty wasn't peeling potatoes like you've probably heard, because they have a machine that does that. But it's still a crap job because you start at four thirty in the morning. The chief cook was surprised to see me. I told him what had happened and I told him the plan.

Part of being on KP is serving when guys come through the line. They slide their trays along that metal rack just like you do in school. It wasn't my job to peel the potatoes, but I had the honor of dishing them up. My friend came through the line and I slapped his potatoes on his tray. Then with great gusto I hacked into them—a great big disgusting mouthful of whatever I could cough up—while he looked on. The thing was, he had to eat it. That was the army way. You had to eat whatever was on your tray, every bite.

I can't be sure that he ate it, of course, because I wasn't around for that. But if he didn't he had to find a place to put a big sloppy pile of mashed potatoes. It wasn't nearly what he had coming, but it made me feel better just the same.

I wasn't in a fighting mood once I got that second speeding ticket under my belt. I knew if I got three speeding tickets within a year, I'd lose my license. I still could barely walk and needed to be able to drive. It's not that I suddenly started paying attention to the speed limit. I never have. But I wasn't necessarily looking to break any records for a while.

Oh sure, I kept racing. One night it was just Duane Opdahl—we called him Dewey—and me. I was making a U-turn when he pulled alongside me. He had a 390 Ford Torino and it

Darlene and I at Fishermen's Wharf in San Francisco, November 1966.

Leaving Minnesota for Vietnam, September 1967. From left: my mom, Arleene; sister Lana; me; twin sister, Cathy; and my dad, Ole.

At base camp, 25th Infantry Division, Cu Chi, Vietnam, November 1967.

Base camp, Cu Chi, Vietnam, November 1967.

Going through the jungle on an APC, November 1967.

Huey helicopters bringing more troops into the field, November 1967.

APCs all lined up at base camp over Christmas, 1967.

The perimeter outside the Filhol Rubber Plantation, where we were clearing trees, November 1967.

Thanksgiving Day menu, Vietnam, November 1967. A welcome break from the C rations.

THANKSGIVING DAY DINNER

Shrimp Cocktail

Crackers

Roast Turkey

Turkey Gravy   Cornbread Dressing   Cranberry Sauce

Mashed Potatoes   Glazed Sweet Potatoes

Buttered Mixed Vegetable

Assorted Crisp Relishes

Hot Rolls   Butter   Fruit Cake   Mincemeat Pie

Pumpkin Pie w/Whipped Topping

Assorted Nuts   Assorted Candy   Assorted Fresh Fruits

Tea w/Lemon   Milk

Leslie Cowden, sitting in the hatch of a medic's track, December 1967.
Photograph courtesy of his mother, Elizabeth Cowden Hiltz.

Richard Godbout, 1967.

My APC, minutes after I was wounded on January 8, 1968. My blood is visible on its side. In the background is track 51, the APC Dick Godbout was riding on when he was killed.

The front of my APC after we got hit. The engine broke through a two-inch solid steel cover and landed fifty yards away, leaving this hole.

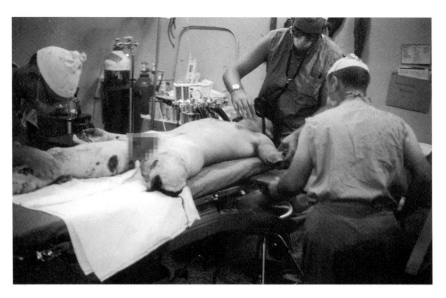

At the 12th Evac Hospital in Cu Chi, Vietnam, shortly after I was wounded.

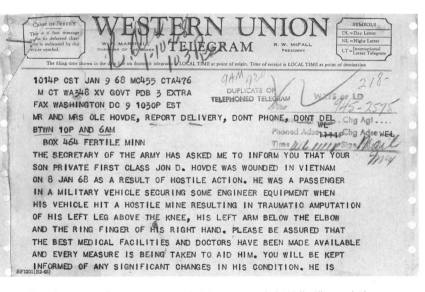

The telegram notifying my parents that I was wounded. Wally Ellegaard, the police chief in Fertile then, delivered it to them about eight o'clock the morning of January 10, 1968. It wasn't entirely accurate: I was the driver of the military vehicle, not a passenger.

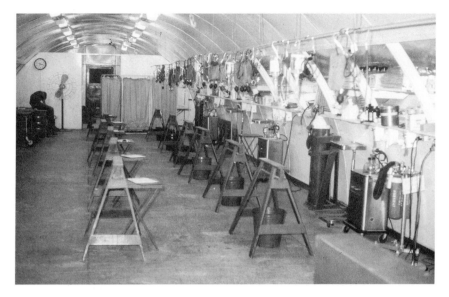

The operating room at the 12th Evac, January 1968.

Stretchers outside the operating room at the 12th Evac, January 1968. The blood has been washed off and they are drying in the morning sun.

Chaplain Donald
Ostroot, 1968.

Father J. E. Vessels, 1968.

Recuperating at Letterman General Hospital, March 1968.

Letterman General Hospital, March 1968. From left: Mom, Dad, Uncle Randy, and me.

The entertainer Barbara McNair visits me at Letterman, March 1968.

Lawrence P. Casey, who played Private Mark Hitchcock in the television show *The Rat Patrol,* visiting me at Letterman, March 1968.

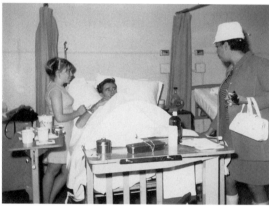

Actress Della Reese visiting me at Letterman, summer 1968. Darlene is on the left.

Darlene and I in June 1969, the day she graduated from high school and one week before we were married.

Clark Dyrud and I at the Vietnam Veterans Memorial on November 12, 1982, the day before it was dedicated. We're pointing to Les Cowden's name.

Clark Dyrud pushing me in a wheelchair down Constitution Avenue in Washington, D.C., on November 13, 1982. We were part of the Minnesota delegation that marched in the parade shortly before the Vietnam Veterans Memorial was dedicated. Photograph courtesy of Gwen Dyrud.

After my speech at the public school in Fosston, Minnesota, circa 1995.

With the Godbout family at their house in Goffstown, New Hampshire, Memorial Day weekend, 2000. Left to right: Dick's brother, Robert Godbout; Dick's widow, Linda; me; and Dick's sister, Cecile. A couple of Dick's nephews are on the right.

Kay Layman and I at our reunion in Albuquerque, New Mexico, on
October 22, 1998—more than thirty years after I got back from the war.

Kay Layman and I at the Fargo Air Museum during Vietnam Week,
May 2004. Photograph courtesy of Charles Gustafson.

was green, the same as my Charger. He rolled down his window and hollered, "Jon! I hear your Charger's pretty fast."

"You heard right," I hollered back. I didn't leave it at that—wouldn't even have known how. "I've never been beaten," I added.

"Okay," Dewey said. "Let's run 'em."

I thought about it.

"I can't," I said. "I have two speeding tickets already."

Dewey looked at me. "Well, yeah," he said. "I know. That car really isn't that fast."

That's all I needed. Rather than go out of town a little bit, like out to the airport—our dinky little airport, about a mile from town—it became so urgent we just tore off right there.

We tromped on it. I was only about a quarter-mile north of Fertile when I was already going seventy, seventy-five. I looked in the rearview mirror and Dewey wasn't alongside me, but he was right on my tail. "Geez," I thought. "That's pretty fast for a Ford." I kept thinking how he was doing better than I expected, and made sure I kept it on the floor. I got past this little tar road that takes you to Beltrami and looked in the rearview mirror again. I started pulling away as I thought, well, I've got him now.

I got up to the Y on the very north end of Fertile. There's a car dealership there now. If you bear right at the Y, the house I live in now is about a mile up the road. If you bear left, you go into Crookston. For some reason, just before the Y, I decided to look in the rearview mirror one more time.

There they were.

Red lights.

"Oh God, I am *dead*," I thought. I just knew it.

I knew how fast I had to have been going. The Charger would do about a 140 miles an hour, top end, if the wind was right.

The officer pulled me over and I kept thinking, I am a dead man.

In those days, you got out of your vehicle and walked back to the squad. This one was an unmarked highway patrol car from Crookston. They had the red lights in the grill in those days. There was no cherry on top, no markings on the door. It was a maroon '69 Plymouth. I will never forget that car.

I got out, but my foot was so sore I had to hang onto the Charger as I worked my way toward the back of it. It took me a while. By now the officer was getting out of his squad. He took one look at me and said, "My God—what happened to you?"

Remember I was twenty years old. All I could think was, opportunity. So I laid it on. He got the goriest version of my story ever told, though I wasn't very far into it when he said, "Jon, I know all about it. I've read about you in the newspaper."

The next thing he wanted to know was who I'd been racing. No way.

I knew he'd want to give Dewey a ticket, too, and that's just not what you did.

"Well," I said. "I think it was *you*."

He didn't laugh. It just made him more mad. But I wasn't mouthing off. I really wasn't. Granted I didn't want to get Dewey in trouble, but by now I was pretty sure it was actually the cop and not Dewey on my tail the whole time.

I only found out a few years ago, when Dewey started getting calls from people who heard this story in speeches I gave, that he'd seen the cop from the start and made a beeline for Beltrami. He parked the car over by his mother's house and hid out.

"By all rights, Jon," the patrolman continued, "I ought to haul you to jail."

"Why would you do that?" I asked him. Again I wasn't lipping off. I genuinely wanted to know. I mean, granted I was speeding, but I didn't think they locked people up for drag racing.

"Do you know how fast you were going?" he replied.

I kind of knew.

"I'm not sure," I said.

And he said, "Jon, I clocked you at 138 in a 55 zone." When he said that, my heart sunk—because he had me. You can sometimes talk your way out of seventy in a fifty-five. But 138! There was no way to get out of this one.

I thought it was over, and I was trying to get used to the idea of losing my license. "I have one last chance," I thought. I knew he had a 440 engine in his Plymouth because that was the biggest engine Chrysler had and it was in all the cop cars. But I asked him, "What engine do you have in that Plymouth?"

"Oh," he said, "I have the 440." He was actually kind of nice when he said that.

So I said, "You know, that thing's pretty slow for a 440. I only have the 383, but it's the high-performance 383."

He seemed to be losing interest. "Yeah," he said. "It is." Pause. "But I have the red lights."

So he wrote me up. If I remember right, he marked it down to ninety. No speeches, nothing. Though he did say I'd have to go to the courthouse.

I got the notice within a week or so, to appear at the courthouse in Crookston. I drove myself there, believe it or not, not really knowing how I'd get home. It wasn't like I was telling a lot of people about this.

I didn't have to appear before a judge. The room they sent me to was pretty bare. All that was in there was a desk and another highway patrolman. I walked in and it seemed like it took forever to drag my thirty-pound leg over to where he was sitting. As soon as I did, he told me to hand over my driver's license. I did, then turned around and headed for the door.

"Just where do you think you're going?" he demanded.

I looked at him. "Sir," I said. "I know the rules. Three tickets in a year and you lose your license. I just happened to do it within a month."

I headed for the door again, but he wasn't finished yelling at me.

"I'm going to give you your license back," he said.

Huh?

"I'm going to give you your license back," he said again, but you are going to come back here and sit down and listen to what I have to say."

I can't remember much of what he said. It was more the way he said it. He chewed my butt bad for at least a half an hour. My drill sergeant in boot camp could chew ass better than anybody I've ever met in my life, but this guy was a close second.

He finally wrapped it up and never once gave me the impression he thought any better of me for keeping my mouth shut and listening. But he kept his word. He handed me back my license, except it had a big paper clip on it. I'd never seen a paper clip that big. I reached for my wallet. "Oh no," he said.

"What do you mean?" I asked.

"Your license is not going back in that wallet," he told me. "This is what the paper clip's for. When you get down to that '68 Charger, I want you to clip this license above your sun visor on the driver's side. And I will tell you this. The next time you look in your rearview mirror and you see red lights, just roll down your window, reach up and get that license and chuck it out the window." He paused. "We have nothing more to talk about."

Again I headed for the door, and again he stopped me.

"Jon," he said, "before you leave I just want you to answer one more question."

I looked at him.

What?

"Why would a guy like you, who's survived all you survived, want to come back and kill yourself on our highway?"

For probably the first time in my entire life, I didn't have an answer.

And it would be more than ten years before I got another ticket.

May Day, 1969. I woke up and thought, well, I've had my party. My parents, who'd shown nothing but patience with my routine of drinking until early morning and sleeping until early afternoon, were starting to wonder about me. More than once they hinted at how there was more to life than the bars, that maybe my life held more promise than that.

Darlene and I had been serious about each other practically from the beginning. She was best friends with my cousin Carol Larson, who was her classmate. We had met while I was working construction with my uncle in Rodeo, California, and were each other's only serious relationship. She was just finishing up her senior year in high school and I thought, well, now's the time.

It was almost like, I need something to help me quit drinking. I know! I'll get married. A wife will put an end to that. But seriously, I loved Darlene and it was time to get on with our lives.

I called. She wasn't home. She was at my uncle's. I called her there and asked her to marry me. Just like that. I may have asked her to sit down first, but it wasn't some flowery speech or anything. She said yes. "Well," I said. "When?" She thought about it for a moment. "How about the first day of summer? June 21? That would be cool." That sounded fine to me.

She ran home to tell her parents the minute we hung up. Her dad was relaxing in his easy chair and thought he'd better not get up. "This is going to cost me a lot of money," he pointed out, and wanted time to get used to the idea. Her mom needed more time. She thought Darlene was too young. Who wouldn't have? It was going to be difficult to watch her only daughter leave home, but she did her best to be supportive. And looking back she says the hardest part was finding a pair of white dress shoes in time.

I sent Darlene a bouquet of sweetheart roses for her birthday, May 11, and soon after that a ring. I went down to Minneapolis to buy the ring so my twin sister, Cathy, could help me pick it out—she worked at a bank downtown. Darlene didn't have any money so I bought my wedding ring, too. Between both wedding rings and her engagement ring it came to more than three hundred bucks—not the two months' salary the diamond commercials try to talk you into spending, but it was still a lot of money.

I mailed Darlene her engagement ring.

My mom and dad couldn't make it out to California for the wedding—it was just too far. It wasn't only the money. My dad's health had continued to deteriorate and it wouldn't have been smart for him to make the trip. My youngest sister, Lana, drove to Rodeo with me about two weeks before the big day.

We said our vows the afternoon of Saturday, June 21, 1969. I was so nervous I could barely get them out, and the minister kept saying "Diane" instead of "Darlene," which upset her. There was a reception at the church and the minister couldn't resist making a comment about how many beer cans were tied behind my car. We went over to Dar's folks' house after that, for champagne, a change of clothes, and the goodbyes.

We honeymooned in San Francisco. I hadn't even made room reservations, that's how dumb I was. When we got into the city and stopped at the first hotel we saw I asked the man at the desk about their honeymoon suite. "Yeah," he said. "I've been waiting for you." "Gee," I thought. "That's odd." Of course the reservation wasn't for us and we took off again. The only place we could find a room was at a motel by Letterman, believe it or not, with two queen-size beds.

Nothing was open the next day, a Sunday, so we had lunch at Kentucky Fried Chicken. We'd already been to San Francisco together so felt no pressure to see the sights—we'd already seen them. Honestly we were glad to get out of there after a couple of days. We went back to Dar's parents' house and packed up her stuff. I hooked a U-Haul to my Charger and off we went. It was hard on the in-laws. It would have been difficult regardless, but Darlene was really young.

She was excited. A new bride, she thought she was taking off on this grand adventure, and I suppose in some ways she was. But she spent much of our first year together in tears because she was so homesick. Even now it gets to her when Christmas approaches. We've only been with her family four times at Christmas, in more than thirty years.

We didn't have much cash in our pockets on our trip back to Fertile and I was such a sucker with what we did have. We had to stop for one reason or another and a guy at this service station took one look at my shocks—or should I say, took one look at *me*—and told me I needed new ones. Now. I had maybe a hundred and thirty dollars, and he took almost all of it. I barely had enough money for gas the rest of the way and there sure as hell wasn't enough for a hotel room. So we drove through the night and got back to Minnesota early in the morning.

I had a little kitten or something for a bank and the first thing I did when we got to my parents' house was break into that. It had about a hundred dollars in quarters. That's what I used to get us into an apartment in New Hope, a suburb of Minneapolis, where we headed after loading up my stuff. I started school at North Hennepin Community College soon after.

That's where the people at the Veterans Administration said I had to attend school. It had to be wheelchair accessible, blah, blah, blah. They said they wanted to make sure I could attend class, and since they were footing the bill I was in no position to argue. I went there for two years before transferring to Moorhead State College, now Minnesota State University-Moorhead.

Our son, Jeremy, was born while we were still in the Twin Cities—June 24, 1970. Jessica came along January 22, 1974; by then we were in Dilworth, just outside of Moorhead. By then they were also letting fathers into the delivery room. When the doctor heard what had happened to me in Nam, he said he didn't think they had to worry about me passing out. It was really something to witness the birth of my daughter. The days our children arrived were two of the proudest of my life.

We had a brand-new, three-bedroom rambler in Dilworth while I was still going to school. Darlene took a few classes at Moorhead State, but for the most part she was a mother and housewife.

I had mostly left any thoughts of the war behind by the time I went to college, or so I told myself. People knew what had happened to me, but nobody said much about it. Unless you're related to or are very close friends with a Vietnam vet, it wasn't something people were eager to bring up in casual conversation. Least of all me. I just didn't think it affected me that much. I had the elevator key to the business hall elevators so I didn't have to use the stairs, but other than that I can't say life was any different for me than it was for other college students.

I was treasurer of the vets' club, and they were kind of a rowdy bunch. They liked to party and I accepted my share of invitations to join them. Darlene always came with, though, and we all had a good time.

I majored in business and finance. I was thinking of becoming a loan officer in a bank or even getting into the stock market somehow. But when I started interviewing for jobs in the Fargo-Moorhead area, I was dismayed to find the pay was so low. "Hey," one banker told me. "We have three colleges in town. These kids get out of school and go back home to live with Mom and Dad. We don't have to pay them that much."

"Geez," I said. "I have a wife and two kids. I can't afford to work for that."

When I first got out of school I wanted to be a prosthetic chief. They're in charge of ordering the new legs for amputees and working with them until they get used to them. But the test you had to take to qualify for that job was filled with all these medical terms I wasn't familiar with. So I went back to business, my original plan.

We loved our house in Dilworth and loved having so much of our family nearby. We had planned on staying, but it was not to be.

By August 1974, I was getting depressed. On a whim I threw a couple of suits in my car one Wednesday. "I'll be back Friday with a job," I told Darlene, before I took off for the Twin Cities.

Yeah right, she thought.

CHAPTER 6

Mr. Businessman

Ready, fire, aim. You'd think a Vietnam vet would be the last person to screw up the sequence of such simple commands. But if I had to sum up the way I operate, it would be with those three words, in that order.

I hadn't approached anyone about a job either by telephone or letter, but I headed for Minneapolis and stayed with my sister and her husband. Thursday morning I went to Control Data, General Mills, and 3M. Somehow I talked my way into interviews at Control Data and 3M, and was heading out the door Friday to go to Pillsbury when my brother-in-law hollered that the phone was for me. It was Jim Stadler from 3M. He'd interviewed me the day before and now he was offering me a job, trade list coordinator, for $10,600 a year. That was almost four thousand dollars more than I could have made in Fargo-Moorhead. "Could you start Monday?" Jim wondered.

"Well," I said, "I have a house to sell."

He asked again. "Do you think you could start Monday?"

I thought about how lucky I'd been to even get an interview, let alone a job.

"Well, yes," I told him. "I guess I can."

I got out of my dress clothes, jumped in my car, and headed home. Darlene was sitting on the front steps of our house talking to a neighbor while the kids played in the yard. "We have to get this house sold!" I hollered out the window. "I start work at 3M Monday!" She laughed. She just thought that was hilarious. Eventually I got through: this wasn't a joke. We figured out what we needed to do. I went back to Minneapolis Sunday while she stayed in Dilworth with the kids. We sold our house within a week and then moved into a townhouse in Eagan.

Trade list coordinator was an entry-level job. Mostly I shuffled paper in the division that sells sandpaper, tape, and so on. I did a lot of filing and also priced special cuts of sandpaper. They referred things like that to me and I figured them out. It was a lot of math. I was also responsible for printing up pricing literature and other materials. It was okay. It got boring after a while, but I knew if I did a good job I could move up.

It wasn't long before the woman who had the job of pricing coordinator got fired and I got her job—my first promotion. I had to ask for it, which surprised me. I finally went into my boss's office and talked to him about the position. It paid more and was more challenging. "I've been waiting for you to come in and ask," he said. And that was it: my next rung on the corporate ladder.

The thing at 3M was that we were supposed to carry around a business card with the job we wanted next written on the back. They wanted you to be always thinking about the job you wanted next, and if a superior happened to ask you what it was, you were supposed to just show them your card. One day my boss put that question to me. "What job do you think you'd like next, Jon?" I showed him my card. On the back I'd written, "Yours." He chuckled and said, "You'll get it. There's no doubt in my mind that you'll get it."

Jim had never gone to college and kind of resented guys who

had. He said it had taken him more than twenty years to get to the level I was at already, and because I had walked in with a college degree, it was mine. He didn't seem to hold it against me, though. I don't know if he felt bad for what I'd been through and what I was still going through. If so, he never let on. We never talked about it.

I hadn't been at 3M very long before they put a picture of my family on the front page of the company newsletter and included a nice story about me inside. They talked about the war in that piece, but there wasn't a lot of room for detail in such a publication.

Looking back it just seemed like everyone knew what had happened to me and nobody talked about it. I certainly didn't. I never talked about Vietnam at 3M; I never even thought about it. I sent my chaplains different things from work because they really liked hearing from me. But those were the only occasions I found myself waxing melancholy about the war.

I don't even know if there were other Vietnam vets at 3M. I guess there might have been, but it just never came up.

My new job consisted mostly of producing pricing literature, and I handled all the pricing for the household hardware products division. I wasn't on that job very long before I got promoted to pricing supervisor, beating out the guy I had previously reported to. I got a 25 percent raise that time. I was moving up.

I never wondered if I got special treatment because I was a veteran. There was nothing said, nothing hinted at, nothing behind my back—and I was as tangled up in the grapevine as anyone else. I despised the politics and yet I was good at it. That's one thing about military life: it's great preparation for corporate life. Managers like good soldiers, and I was a good soldier. There was many a time when one of them noticed just how many hours I was putting in and suggested I cut back because I was making everyone else look bad.

But I didn't know how to cut back. I didn't know how to go at something at less than full speed. Still don't, I guess.

I was so hung up on getting ahead it almost embarrasses me, because even then I think I knew better. Even then I would joke about the new title I'd just been handed. "Titles are like assholes," I'd say. "Everybody has one."

Not that I didn't go after the next promotion—I always did. I deluded myself into thinking I was just keeping my second vow, that's all. I wasn't going to be dependent on the government. I was going to be a productive member of society. I was going to be a *very* productive member of society.

I didn't know it until I was no longer with 3M, but apparently it had gone straight to the top management how many hours I put in evenings and weekends. If you came into the building on, say, a Saturday, you placed your pass on a screen, and once the pass was scanned the guards would click the door to let you in. And somehow there was a record of who'd been putting in time, and how much, outside the normal workweek.

I didn't find this out until after I left the company, but when you're at 3M, if you get a pay increase every nine months, you're considered a Grade A employee. The average employee got a pay increase after twelve months, and if you were on an eighteen-month schedule, word was you should be looking for another job. I never went longer than nine months without a raise, and they were anywhere from 7 to 25 percent.

I don't doubt that my disability and the fact that I was a veteran got my, uh, one foot in the door with the company, but it was just that, a foot in the door. After that I was on my own. I busted my tail and no one questioned how quickly I was moving up.

My right foot continued to give me fits. The pain never stopped. As useful as I felt at work, I was useless once I got home—Darlene can tell you. I had to lie on the couch every night and keep my foot raised for two or three hours at least. It throbbed like your worst toothache. It was like that from my very first day at 3M because I did that much walking. Even now I need to see a doctor every three weeks to carve away at the bone that grows right out of the skin on my heel. It's almost like a really hard callus or wart. It doesn't hurt so much anymore—it's almost like trimming a fingernail—but back then it killed me. And that was the least of my problems as far as the foot was concerned.

I was too stubborn to use a wheelchair at 3M, but I probably should have. Remember, my foot was a scrambled egg, and there was no fixing it. The most I could hope for was that it wouldn't get worse, but walking around all day made it worse. I wasn't just sitting at my desk pushing paper, after all. I was always walking to this building or that—my jobs were at corporate headquarters in St. Paul, a huge campus—or rushing to this or that meeting. And I didn't want to be in a wheelchair any more than anyone else would.

I was always on the move, even at lunch. In fact the thing that stands out the most about my time at 3M was being in the cafeteria with my boss and my boss's boss. I was carrying my tray with a bowl of chili on it near a sign that said, "Wet Floor." No kidding. Next thing I knew I was flat on my back, looking right into my boss's eyes.

"Oh my God," he said, "Are you hurt?" It was hard to process the question because he was laughing his head off.

"I'm okay, I think," I told him.

"I'm sorry, Jon," he added. "I know this isn't funny, but . . ."

"What happened?" I said.

"You're not going to believe this," he said, "but your shoe, your sock, and your *foot* are right behind you."

I was so embarrassed.

You think that's funny? I hadn't spilled a drop of chili. Not one drop.

My left foot had literally come off. In those days the bottom part of my leg was still made out of wood, and the foot was bolted to that. I'd been doing a lot of boating at the time. I'd get that sucker wet, the wood would expand and contract, and eventually the nut loosened up and fell off. So this day when I took a step, it left my foot—and everything attached to it—behind.

"What do we do?" Jim asked. He was still horrified, you could tell.

"Well, first thing," I said, "I need a wheelchair. Then if someone would please go get my foot. . . . " Someone wheeled me to my car, and I headed to the limb shop to get my foot put back on.

It was always something. I was into boating whenever I could tear myself away from work, but swimming wasn't in the cards. I only tried it once. I swim like a Daredevil. You know those red-and-white Daredevls, the fishing lures? They spiral through the water as you pull them along. That's what happens to me when I try to swim without a life jacket. Without an arm and a leg on my left side, I just spin around.

I'm better at golf. You two-armed folks probably aren't impressed that I can drive a golf ball a hundred and sixty-five yards, but it thrills me. And I keep improving. One guy said my swing would improve if I'd just pivot a little more on my left foot. I had a little fun with him. "But I don't *have* a left foot." You should have seen his face.

The cafeteria incident, as it came to be known, was about as exciting as it got at 3M. The corporate life was boring, but it was also all-consuming. I was killing myself at a job that really didn't have a lot of meaning—like a lot of people do, I suppose. You'd think going off to war would give you a perspective on what's really important, that you wouldn't get all caught up in things that, looking back, I can see were superficial. But I did.

So much so that I'd sum up this part of my life in three words: Ethan Allen furniture.

I had started at 3M in August 1974 and after about five years with the company things began to unravel. It started one day when I was walking through a nursery over lunch with a colleague. It was spring and I was buying flowers for the house. Suddenly I felt something snap in my back. I thought I'd pulled a muscle. It kept hurting and getting worse. I limped around for three days—I came into work as usual, of course—before my boss insisted that I have a doctor check it out.

I had popped a disk and there was really nothing they could do except sever it from my spine. I checked into the VA hospital and by the time they got me into a bed I couldn't get back up again, that's how bad I was getting by the minute.

I was out of work for a month after that. They didn't fuse my spine back together, but instead just cut the disk loose and let it float. I was only thirty-two then, and the feeling was that you should put off back surgery as long as you possibly could. It worried me. I wondered how I'd walk, being an amputee and all. I already had a limp, though I learned that having the limp was probably the reason I had back troubles to begin with.

My wooden leg was probably three-quarters of an inch shorter than my right leg. They could have matched it exactly, but if it's just a little bit shorter, the toe doesn't get hung up when I swing it and it's easier to keep from tripping. Also, if the wooden leg's a little shorter you don't have to drag it. Without a knee, if something goes wrong, you're on your face.

Walking was hell on my back. In those days, prosthetic legs were very heavy. Just dragging that much extra weight was a killer, and it's not like I could go on a diet to lose it.

The doctor at the VA had said that it probably wouldn't be a problem to just leave the disk in there, and it really hasn't been. Over all these years, my back has been the least of my troubles. There have been a few times when I've popped something and been down for six or seven days, but that has only happened once every five years or so. I can more or less lift heavy stuff, too. The problem is when I twist in a funny way. If I do a lot of walking I usually use a cane because it helps to straighten my back. I hate using a cane—no surprise there. But it's not just vanity. If you're carrying anything at all it gets awkward in a hurry.

I was in the hospital for two of the four weeks I was off work and spent the other two weeks at home.

It didn't occur to me that my health problems had anything to do with my breakneck pace. I never really thought of myself as having an addictive personality, but there were obvious signs. First there was the dependence on alcohol to get me through the worst of the reentry into so-called normal life after the war. And most recently there was the workaholism. Nobody sets you up as a hero if you drink a lot, but working a lot usually commands respect, unless you're the wife or child being shortchanged. They weren't complaining, though, and I went blindly along. I kept thinking about myself and my career. It was selfish, no doubt, the one-track mind. I had a dictaphone and I dictated letters to and from work. I was always working, or thinking about work, which may explain why the people at 3M were so accommodating when it came to my back problems. Among other things, they bought me a special chair and got me a headset so I didn't have to cradle the phone.

In May 1979, about a year after my back went out, my foot suddenly got a lot worse. It had always been practically unbearable, so that's saying a lot. There was white pus coming out of the bottom of it, and I was still wrestling with the bone spur growing out of the bottom of my heel. I kept it in check by kind of carving at it by myself. Once in a while a doctor looked at it, but there wasn't much anyone could do.

No one seemed to know what was causing this latest trouble. My heel kept draining until finally I decided to visit the medical director at 3M. He took one look at it and said, "I don't know what that stuff is, but we have to get you in to see some orthopedic people." He sent me to some orthopedic surgeons who were supposed to be really good. They took a culture and told me it was infected. I wasn't surprised. I remembered how standard it was for VC to urinate and defecate on mines before they planted them, and I was sure some bug had been in my bone tissue since the day I was wounded.

They called in an infection specialist, who took another culture and told me I had four different infections of my heel bone— all acute. One doctor wanted to try an antibiotic to see if it would kill them, but we knew it would have to be a pretty powerful one. So get this: he sent the culture to Eli Lilly in Indianapolis and they developed a special drug just for me. They predicted with 99 percent certainty that it would kill the infection.

The surgeons had shaved off a piece of bone and it was still draining. Someone brought in a little box of pills, which was the antibiotic; they were going to crush it, put it into IV form, and inject it into me. There were also a couple of little vials. When I asked the doctor what was in them he said, "Adrenalin."

"What are you going to do with that?" I asked.

"Well, Jon," he said, "this antibiotic they've developed is so powerful there's a possibility you could have an allergic reaction to it. If you do, I'm going to stick one of those vials of Adrenalin in you to get you going again."

"Why are there two?" I asked.

"Because if I have to put one in you," he said, "I'm going to have to put the other one in me." To this day I could swear he wasn't kidding.

I was in the hospital for all this. After the doctor started the first IV, I was told, the antibiotic started working within about five minutes. I had to have it dropped into me every twelve hours over a four- or five-day period. The doctor sat with me for a good hour and nothing happened, so I thought everything was fine. About two o'clock the next morning they came in with my second dose. I was awake for that, and after the nurse started that IV she left the room, but I literally saw the air move out with her. It was eerie. I couldn't breathe! I hit the button for the nurse and she came running. "What's the matter?" she asked.

"I can't breathe!" I told her. Within two minutes my doctor was there with a whole team of people.

He took a needle and of course I had only my right arm to shove it into; when he did I could see the blood bubbling in the syringe. I asked him what he was doing and he said he was taking a sample to find out how much oxygen was in my blood. "I think you just had a nasty allergic reaction," he said.

He took that vial and in front of so many people he handed it to a guy who got a preemptive butt chewing: "You tell those folks in the lab I want these results back in five minutes, and if I don't get them that fast I will be down there myself with a dull needle to take some blood out of *them*."

The guy took off in a dead run.

The results were back within five minutes, and the oxygen level in my blood was really low. How low I don't remember, but it was critical so they gave me a shot of something to counteract the effect the antibiotic was having on me.

After this ordeal was over, my doctor said he wanted to take the whole heel bone because it was still infected, of course, and trying the antibiotic again was out of the question. "If I do it again it will kill you," he said. "Period."

"It's a sad deal," he added, "because your foot's going to be pretty slushy without any heel bone. But that's the only way to get rid of the infection, to take the whole bone."

I decided to get a second opinion. I went to see a doctor at another hospital and he took a circular saw to the side of my foot. He opened it on the bottom and the side, maybe thinking it would let more of the nasty stuff drain out.

Usually I'm all over any doctor, wanting to be told exactly what they're doing and why. But I was distracted. I was still doing my 3M job from the hospital bed and I was always on the phone, trying to run things from there. I had lost about twenty-five pounds by then, and really wasn't holding up as well as I thought I was.

One night the doctor who had treated me to begin with showed up at the hospital and looked at my chart. "Oh my God," he said. "Do you know who was in the operating room?" He couldn't believe what they'd done to me.

"No," I said. "They knocked me out before I got in there."

Normally I would not only have known who was operating on me, but what he was operating *with*. It had become a game, to have someone lift the white sheet covering the tools they were going to use. I could tell what they were going to do to me by what was under there. Depending on what I saw—like saws, for example—I'd think, "Oh God, *this* one's going to hurt."

I had no idea who had been going at me this last time, or with what.

"They only took half the heel bone!" he said. "What were they thinking? They have to take the whole thing!" It wasn't just part of the bone that was infected, he said, it was the whole thing.

"This isn't going to work," he said, his voice trailing off.

Somebody told me later that the doctor who'd done the cutting was selling jewelry in Arizona. If anyone should have been sued, I suppose it was him, but that's not my style.

My foot continued draining after I left the hospital. Darlene changed the dressings, but it was tough on her because she could actually see my heel bone sticking through the skin on my foot.

A few days after I got home we noticed how red the foot was getting. By now it was Christmas and Darlene's folks had just flown in to stay with us. I went back to the first doctor, who said, "Well, that's what happens when you leave half the heel bone in there. The infection isn't going to go away." Pause. "I have to open that up."

"So I have to go back into the hospital?" I asked.

"No," he answered. "I can do it right here."

The nurse looked at him with eyes as wide as mine.

"What do you mean, you're going to open it up right here?" I said.

"Well, I'm just going to make a cut in it to take the pressure off."

"You can't do that," the nurse said. "This isn't an operating room. We don't have an operating room." I was surprised and thankful she was challenging him.

They kept going back and forth about whether he could cut into me there and he won. He gave me some kind of shot to numb the area, but it hardly numbed it at all. He came at me with this knife and—no lie—cut the side and bottom of my foot. Blood squirted out and hit the wall and I just about jumped off the table. He cut some more and slid this hose through the bottom of my foot. I was awake through it all—can you imagine? The nurse turned to face the wall. She couldn't take it. I thought I was going to pass out.

The nurse said to me, in front of him, "He should *not* be doing this. Do not let him get away with this." I wasn't used to having a nurse challenge a doctor ever, let alone right in front of my face.

The doctor tried to patch me up and instead just made everything worse. I had to go back into the hospital again, this time to recover from the fix-it job. I was given shots of morphine while various people kept watch and hoped my foot would start to improve somehow. It didn't. I went home to recuperate even though there didn't seem to be any chance of that. Darlene started in again, packing it in fresh dressings and wondering with the rest of us what was going on.

The surgeon told me there was nothing else he could do.

"Well, what the hell," I thought. "I'll just go back to work." I called my boss to talk things over. We had it all planned. They were going to have a nurse available to change my dressing over the lunch hour.

At six-thirty one of the first mornings I was home again I put my suit on to go to work. I was resigned to the wheelchair by then, and wheeled out the back door to the garage. All of a sudden something spun me around. Darlene had grabbed the back of the wheelchair and was wheeling me back into the dining room.

"Just where do you think you're going?" she asked, as if I were a child who had been grounded and been caught trying to escape.

"I have to go back to work," I told her, stunned. It wasn't like Darlene to take me to task like this.

She looked at me.

"Jonny," she said, getting softer. "Why are you trying to kill yourself?"

Huh?

"Why are you killing yourself?" she asked again.

I looked at my foot, then back at her.

"Do you think I'm doing this on purpose?"

"Do you think you have nothing to do with what's happening?" she fired back. "What is this all about, anyway? This brand-new Cape Cod, these new cars, this new boat?" Pause. "All this Ethan Allen furniture?"

I was still too stunned to say anything.

"Why are you trying to kill yourself?" she asked again. "And for whom?"

"I can't just sit here," I said. She was doing her best to get through to me gently, but it still felt like I was being scolded. Though as hardheaded as I am, I also knew there was a possibility she had a point.

All those months preparing for the war, all the ugliness that followed, all the recovery time—and it took Darlene to point out what mattered in life and what didn't.

"The kids are having trouble in school," she said. Did she really think I needed a reminder of *that*? I asked. "Yes, I do," she snapped. "We almost lost you when you had that allergic reaction and the kids are left to wonder if you're going to pull through it—and I'm beginning to wonder how much more *I* can take."

I didn't have to go back very far to see what she meant. In only the last few days the doctors had been warning me that they were going to have to amputate my foot if it didn't stop draining. "You have to do it before the infection moves up the knee," I had told them. My other leg was gone above the knee and that would make it really difficult to get around no matter what they rigged up. I'd have to go to hand controls in my car, for one thing, and that was probably the least of it.

The minister had even come to our house to help us decide what to do.

"What do you want?" I asked Darlene.

"I don't want you to kill yourself anymore," was all she offered.

"Then I need to leave 3M," I said.

She nodded.

"We need to move to California or back to Fertile," I said.

"Okay," she said.

"Want to put it to a vote?" I asked. It was straight out of *The Sound of Music*. Maybe we should ask . . . the children.

We got the kids ready for school, but before they left we talked. Jeremy was eleven and Jessica was seven. I told them I needed to take some time off work to try to help my foot heal, but I didn't want to stay in the Twin Cities without a job. "It's Fertile or California," I said.

The vote was three to one, Fertile. Darlene voted for California.

The people at 3M didn't take the news very well. I called my boss right after the family vote and he said, "You're kidding me." No, I'm not, I assured him. I told him I had to leave, I just did. "I'm going to send a counselor out to talk to you first," he said. "Will you talk to him?" I said I'd talk, but I wasn't going to change my mind.

I knew the counselor. I'd worked with him before. "You don't want to do this, Jon," he said. He was wrong.

"If my right foot doesn't stop draining they're going to amputate," I explained. "I'm already a double amp. I don't want to be a triple amp." He suggested I take more time to think about it.

"I'm running out of time," I countered. "I've been in and out of the hospital for five months, and the only thing that changes is that it keeps getting tougher on my family. I have to try something else."

We put the house up for sale the very next day, in a market where interest rates were pushing 21 percent, and we sold it in a week.

My friends at 3M wanted to throw me a party, which I tried to talk them out of, but couldn't. We went out to lunch together at a restaurant not far from company headquarters. When it was over the vice president of the division, a West Pointer who didn't usually show up for goodbye luncheons, came over and put his arm on my shoulders. "Jon," he said, "only you know what's best for you. But I'll tell you this, if you ever decide you want to come back to 3M, don't screw around with the personnel department. You call me on a Friday, and you start Monday."

That made it easier to leave, knowing I could come back.

Then he gave me another lovely parting gift. When I left the hospital I had bills approaching forty thousand dollars for my foot. The VA wouldn't cover all of it because I hadn't been at a VA hospital; 3M had wanted me somewhere else. My share of the bill was going to be five or six thousand dollars. Before I could even start worrying about it, the vice president told me to stop because 3M would take care of it. I was surprised. I knew the company insurance didn't cover war injuries. But he told me there was a group that took care of special needs not covered by company insurance. He was chair of that committee, he brought my case before it, and he told anyone who disagreed with him that they didn't have to be on the committee anymore.

I went back to Fertile while Darlene attended to the details of getting us moved. I eventually bought ten acres of land just north of town and we made plans to build a house on it and raise quarter horses.

I didn't know how I was going to make a living once we got settled in Fertile, but I didn't worry about it, not one bit. We made more than forty thousand dollars when we sold the house in Apple Valley, our last home in the Cities, so I knew we could live comfortably—at least for a while—without my having to work much at all. I was going to get disability from 3M, $550 a month. I was getting Social Security on top of that, plus my comp. So we'd be okay.

All I wanted at that moment was to get my health and family back.

My last day at 3M was in April 1981. Within two weeks, the draining in my foot had stopped. It was so gradual I didn't even really notice since I was so busy going back and forth between Apple Valley and Fertile, looking for land to buy. I hadn't noticed it wasn't even red anymore. "What are you doing differently?" the latest doctor wanted to know.

"Well," I told her, "I left my job."

Her jaw dropped. "You're kidding," she said. And then, "I think you just saved your foot by doing that." Turns out she had wanted to suggest I quit, but knew I might resent her forever. "Given it was your decision," she added, "that's a whole different story."

Tell me about it. Darlene has said many times that had I stayed at 3M, I would not be alive today. She may have a point.

I not only saved my foot.

I saved my life.

CHAPTER 7

After the Wall

I waited more than fifteen years to say goodbye to Dick Godbout. I was prepared to wait forever. Nothing against Dick, but I couldn't think about him without thinking about the war, and I didn't see the point. I'd been to Vietnam and had no interest in going back, literally or figuratively.

Everything changed when I started reading about the Vietnam Veterans Memorial in Washington, D.C. I thought it was a good idea. It would be a chance for people like me to say goodbye to our friends. I wanted to visit it someday, but I had no intention of going to the dedication, which was planned for Saturday, November 13, 1982.

I had belonged to American Legion Post 238 since I was wounded, and one day the state commander and the ninth district commander came to town. They said four veterans from Minnesota had been selected to attend the dedication and I was one of them. So was Clark Dyrud, my old squad leader from Vietnam; by then he was a veterans claims representative for the state of Minnesota, working out of Moorhead. Most of our expenses were paid by the legion and the rest would be minimal since the four of us were going to stay with Clark's brother in Laurel, Maryland.

We left for D.C. from Minneapolis and shortly after takeoff the pilot came on and said he had an announcement. "We have the honor of having a lot of Vietnam veterans on this plane," he said, "who are going to our nation's capital for the dedication of the Vietnam Veterans Memorial." You should have heard the applause. I basked in it, I must admit. There hadn't been a lot of that kind of thing since I had returned from the war.

People were just beginning to come around where Vietnam was concerned. Whatever their personal feelings about our country's involvement, many seemed suddenly willing to put those aside long enough to say a simple thank you to those of us who had served. More and more I got the feeling that the general population was eager to give veterans of Vietnam the same respect given to veterans of other wars. Had it not been for my limp, I would have straightened my shoulders and walked with my head held a little higher.

The applause was such a pleasant surprise I felt like raising a little hell. I wondered how many veterans were on board. "I wonder if these guys remember cadence," I said, looking at Clark. About that fast, something just came over me. I belted one out:

I knew a girl who lived on the hill.
She wouldn't do it but her sister will.

Clark, God bless him, wasn't going to let me die. He piped right in.

Sound off. One, two.

Just like that, some others joined in.

Sound off. Three, four.

I couldn't believe how many veterans were on this plane.
Because we were getting louder and louder.

Bring it on down.
One, two.
Three, four.

Okay, let's see if I can remember another one.

I left my home in a Chevrolet.
Now I'm walking all the way.

It sounded like half the people on board were singing now.

Sound off. One, two.
Sound off. Three, four.

Voices were bouncing off every corner of the plane.

Bring it on down.
One, two, three, four.
One, two. THREE, FOUR!

Okay, let's see.

I know a girl who's dressed in black.
She makes her living on her back.
Sound off. One, two.
Sound off. Three, four.
Bring it on down.
One, two, three, four.
One, two, THREE, FOUR!

This wasn't the beer talking—er, singing. This was a plane-load of soldiers on a mission. Except this time it would be a mission of healing.

It wasn't just veterans on the plane, but those who weren't didn't seem to mind the commotion. To the contrary. The pilot came back on and said something nice, though I've long since forgotten what it was. The stewardesses sealed that sentiment by bringing us free drinks for getting everyone so fired up.

I was excited to see Washington, D.C. I'd never been there before. I kept my nose pressed to the window like a little kid. We could see the Capitol from the air as we circled, but it was toward evening when we landed, so it was difficult to see as much as I wanted.

We got to Clark's brother's house in plenty of time for dinner. They had a beautiful house, and the Chinese food they ordered tasted so good. We enjoyed the dinner and the conversation but went to bed early. It was going to be a big day. Not the dedication—that was to be the day following. Tomorrow was our first trip to the Wall.

I was still in the shower the next morning when the folks from WDAY Television in Fargo called to ask about an interview. Clark said fine, but I didn't want to be interviewed. I wasn't there for the attention—I wasn't there for anybody else. To me this was personal. I just wanted to say goodbye to my friends. Plus I knew I'd probably be pretty emotional. I'm no different from most men in that I'm self-conscious when I cry. The last thing I wanted was my blubbering face plastered all over television screens back home.

It was suggested to us that since the legion had helped get us there, we should probably say a few words. And what was I going to do? I said okay, but not to expect much.

We took a cab to Potomac Park. Vietnam vets were getting dollar cab rides for those few days, and one cab driver didn't charge us anything. It was cool for Washington, so we had jackets on.

And there it was.

The Vietnam Veterans Memorial is a hundred and forty panels of black Indian granite nestled among all things symbolic: the United States Capitol, the Washington Monument, and the Lincoln and Jefferson Memorials. It's L-shaped, two hundred and seventy-five feet in each direction, and the first panel isn't very high. At its apex, it's about ten feet high, and then it descends gradually to the same shallow height on the other end. It's lower into the ground at that apex as well, and because of its design, it's almost eerie how quiet it is there.

The names of every Vietnam veteran killed or missing in action are etched into the Wall, in the order of the date they were killed, as opposed to alphabetically. The first panel has names of people killed in 1959, believe it or not. That's when the first advisors were sent over. The last panel has the names of those killed in 1975.

They had just laid sod, so the ground was kind of wet and mucky. It was going to be a mess, I guessed, by the time all these people trampled on it.

The first name I looked for was Leslie L. Cowden. He was the reason I was still here. He'd been badly burned saving me and was awarded the Bronze Star for his trouble. He never got the medal because he was killed on the third of February, 1968, less than a month after I was wounded. I send flowers to Les's mom, who still lives in Anoka, every year on February 3, though I forgot last year and it still bothers me. I love that woman. I call her my other mom.

I knew where to find Cowden's name—panel 37E. I had a book with the names in alphabetical order and the panel you could find them on. I made my way through the crowd—what a crowd!—and approached 37E, row 8, my heart racing. The names were all a blur at first, and then I saw it.

Leslie L. Cowden.

There he was. The man who saved my life.

Leslie L. Cowden.

All that was left of him were thirteen letters on a black granite wall. How does that happen? How is it that I was here, and he was there?

There were so many people swirling around, but for a moment it was just Cowden and me. I was looking at the black granite, but all I could see were trees. The granite was so shiny the trees behind us were reflected in it. The day was glorious, not a cloud. And I was in some strange place between heaven and earth, surrounded by all the angels who had saved my life.

The trees were rustling, so their reflection rustled, too. It seemed as if the Wall were moving, as if it were alive.

This is what church is supposed to feel like. I was overcome with a sense of reverence.

Okay, Cowden. Check. I knew Godbout's name would probably be on the panel just to the left of the one with Cowden's, because he'd been killed about a month before. Yeah. There it was. Richard G. Godbout. Panel 33E, row 2.

I took a moment, and said goodbye to my friend.

"Remember Wylie Phillips and William Markle?" Clark said. "And Scott Cook? They were killed the night Godbout died." Oh yeah, that's right. They'd been transferred into our outfit just before they were killed and I hadn't even met them.

William C. Markle, Jr.

Wylie O. Phillips.

Scott H. Cook.

Clark and I just stood there for a minute or two, talking

about the day I got wounded. Suddenly he remembered details that he hadn't thought about in almost fifteen years. He got going and then I found myself remembering things I hadn't before. It seemed like the Wall was pulling them out of us.

And the tears. So many tears. Clark didn't cry, but I couldn't stop. I didn't even bother to try.

What the heck is going on? I wondered. It felt like we were surrounded by spirits who weren't going to let this opportunity pass. We finally had a shoulder to cry on and the tears flowed.

The spell was broken as quickly as it had descended. In no time at all the stringer for WDAY appeared. He wanted our reaction. I'd barely had time to have a reaction, but those were the breaks. So I told him the same thing I've been saying since Vietnam. That if there's ever a hero of a war, his name is etched on a granite wall. I can't remember what else I said. Probably not much.

They interviewed Clark, but not the other two guys we'd made the trip with, Peter Thompson and Roger Bengtson. Clark and I served together, of course, but I was a magnet for cameras. The reporters saw me limping and made their way over. Then they saw my hook and started pushing people out of the way. I felt like the grand champion prize pig at the Minnesota State Fair.

I got stopped by someone from the *Boston Globe* next and did a short interview for them. Then I got stopped by someone from another big newspaper. Same thing. "Let's go," I told Clark. "We have to get out of here. I don't want to do any more of these."

My life was suddenly no longer my own. I hadn't come here to do interviews, and it was ruining the experience. How do you stuff into a sound bite what you feel about the war, your friends, your life? It made me mad that I was being asked to try.

My indignation kept me from crying during the interviews, and I was glad about that.

Some hotels in the area got into the spirit of helping Vietnam veterans, in that each had a board where you could post your name and what outfit you were with. Other guys from your outfit might see your name and be able to hook up however you suggested. By now I knew that almost everyone in my outfit had been killed or wounded, and I was eager to find any who had survived. Supposedly there were 150,000 people in town for this event. Surely someone else from our outfit would have made it to the dedication.

Of course I would also have loved to talk to any of the doctors or nurses who treated me, especially Nurse Kay. I had thought of her often in fourteen years, and was eager to find her somehow.

We went from hotel to hotel, leaving our names and Clark's brother's phone number.

Eventually we also went back to the Wall to check for still more names and take our time there. There were fewer reporters there then, though this was when Gary Gilson shot some video of me. Gary is the executive director of the Minnesota News Council, but back then he had a show on Twin Cities Public Television called *Night Times Magazine* and he had come to tape the dedication for that. He had lost a friend in Vietnam. I was glad to be included on the show. I liked Gary, maybe because he was from Minnesota, maybe because he'd lost someone, too, but I didn't feel like I was being interviewed as much as just talking to a friend. He later told me this particular installment of *Night Times Magazine* was the most requested thing he's ever done.

Next on the agenda was meeting up with the legion people responsible for us having made the trip. We got together at a bar in Georgetown and partied into the night. We didn't talk about the war that much. There were a lot of civilians in the bar and actually we talked about the war more with them than with each other. They were curious about the parade and everything else on tap for the next day.

We took a cab back to Laurel, which cost us about eighty bucks. That was a little outside the radius of dollar rides.

The next day was the big one. It was kind of a gray day, cool for Washington, and first up was the parade. Every state was represented by some of their Vietnam veterans, and General Westmoreland—the grand marshal—was supposedly going to be riding in a convertible toward the front. We were told this was the largest parade and the largest gathering of people since the Kennedy inauguration.

My foot was on the mend, but I knew I wasn't going to be able to walk for two or three miles down Constitution Avenue so I accepted an offer of a wheelchair for that. It was delivered right to the start of the parade route.

Before the parade Westmoreland made his way through the crowd and shook everyone's hand—I mean absolutely everyone's. It took forever. He was a controversial figure. Word was that he had kind of lived in his little cocoon in Saigon and had had food flown in every day. Who knows if that's even true.

To me he was just another rah-rah politician. So when it was my turn to exchange a few words with the big guy, I asked him if he was going to be in some convertible somewhere. Well, no, as a matter of fact, he wasn't. He was going to be on the ground walking with veterans. But I got my dig in.

As we walked by the grandstand, planes flew over in broken formations, then the helicopters came. There weren't any floats, but the number of bands more than made up for that. Clark and I were in the front of the Minnesota delegation—Clark was pushing my wheelchair—and the states were lined up in alphabetical order.

The mood was jubilant. One guy practically skipped into line as he announced, "This sure beats the blank stares I got when I got off the airplane!" I didn't realize that until weeks later, when I saw the Gilson footage.

Afterward, a boy, I'm guessing he was six years old, came up to me when I was still in my wheelchair. His mom said he just wanted to shake my hand and thank me. I hugged the little guy as I shook his hand, then gave him the flag I had waved in the parade. You should have seen his eyes light up. As they walked away I heard him tell his mom, "That man gave me his only flag."

After the parade came the dedication. It was as meaningful as it was brief. President Reagan was out of town, so Secretary of Defense Caspar Weinberger did the honors. His words are as permanently etched in my memory as the names of my friends are etched on the Wall:

> When your country called you, you came.
> When your country refused your honor, you remained silent.
> With time our nation's wounds have healed.
> We have finally come to appreciate your sacrifices and pay you the
>   tribute you so richly deserve.
> Welcome home.

You want to make a Vietnam vet cry? Say those words. I've never met one who didn't lose it.

There were a few more words by someone else, and maybe still someone else, and then somebody said: "And this memorial is dedicated. . . ."

The whole thing probably didn't take ten or fifteen minutes.

We didn't go back to the Wall after the dedication. There were just too many people and it would have been difficult to maneuver through the crowd in a wheelchair, so we left. That was fine with me. I was getting worn out.

We checked back at the hotels we'd been to yesterday, hoping to hook up with someone else from our outfit. Still no luck.

Three thousand veterans had been invited to a reception that night at the American Legion Hall in Washington. It was a huge ballroom, and the place was packed. What struck me was how many amputees there were. Also, no officers. It was just guys who fought the war. I was in the back of the room scoping out the hors d'oeuvres and beer—on the house, of course.

Wolfman Jack was the master of ceremonies. He had a couple of turntables for playing records and kept a half gallon of Windsor—with the cap off—at the little table where he was sitting. He wanted to make this a real party, that was obvious. We heard he'd flown in from California and wasn't getting paid a dime for his appearance. He wanted to play all the oldies for us—you know, "Paint It Black" and some of those.

I hadn't been standing there very long when this guy came up to me after noticing my hook. "When were you wounded?" he asked. "Eighth of January, '68," I said.

"You ought to meet my brother, Gary," he said. "He lost an arm, too."

"I probably will before the night's over."

"Well, I'd like you to meet him now."

I didn't understand the urgency, but he wouldn't let up. What's the harm? I thought. I went with him. I made my way to the front of the room, just to the left of where Wolfman Jack had camped out.

"This is my brother, Gary," my new friend said, before introducing me to Gary Wetzel.

"When were you hit, Jon?" he asked, as he extended his hand for me to shake.

"Eighth of January, '68," I said again.

He looked at me. Instead of shaking my hand he grabbed me and hugged me with such force he squeezed another bucket of tears out of me. We were both crying, but I didn't know why. Oh man, I thought, I've already had a rough day. I'd been crying practically since arriving in D.C. I was hoping to kick back a little.

"What do you think of the Wall?" Gary asked.

I gave him my standard reply, about how heroes are those whose names are etched in granite.

"Amen, brother," he said.

He introduced me to a couple of his friends, Sammy Davis and Robert O'Malley, and there were more hugs—and tears—all around.

We got acquainted. Wetzel had been a door gunner on an army helicopter. Davis was a sergeant in the army, O'Malley a sergeant in the marines.

Wolfman Jack opened his microphone. A song had just ended. He said we had the honor of having some Congressional Medal of Honor recipients with us.

Geez, I thought. That's really something. I knew only about 245 had been awarded to Vietnam veterans, about 100 of them posthumously, so I doubted there were even 100 of them still alive. To get even three here would be pretty amazing.

I'd like to come down here and give a hug and a kiss to every damn one of you, Wolfman Jack continued, but that isn't possible. But will the Congressional Medal of Honor recipients please come on stage?

I couldn't believe it. Gary and his two friends started unbuttoning their shirts to pull out their Congressional Medal of Honor medallions, hanging from ribbons around their necks.

You're kidding, I thought. How did I ever get hooked up with these guys?

Gary went up on stage, along with Sammy. But Bob, the other one, stayed back with us. Gary took the microphone and started singing "God Bless America." A few thousand vets singing that a cappella—I still get chills just thinking about it.

Then it was Sammy's turn. He said what I had heard so

often, that he didn't think he was a hero. He just found himself in a bad situation and tried to fight his way out like the rest of us.

Bob stayed down by me. He was in the marines and was a little guy. "You really should go up there," I said, as gently as I could.

"I can't, Jon," he said. "I'm so shy. . . ."

I wasn't the only one who thought Bob should be on stage. Somebody else grabbed him and told him he should get up there. Suddenly out of nowhere two more men, in trenchcoats, came up to the guy who'd grabbed Bob.

"Don't you touch him," they warned, pulling him off Bob and escorting him away. "He doesn't have to do anything he doesn't want to do." He backed off and I never saw him after that.

The men in trenchcoats must have been Secret Service. I say that because Congressional Medal of Honor recipients are a very big deal. I think these days they're paid about a thousand dollars a month extra. It's the most prestigious medal awarded to veterans and it's the only medal that's protected—you can't buy one.

So O'Malley continued to stand there, and I continued to try to talk him into going on stage, albeit more carefully than ever, given what I'd just witnessed. "You really ought to get up there," I said again, quietly.

I was such a chickenshit back then I should have been ashamed of myself for pushing him. I would never have done what I was asking him to do. But something had come over me and I didn't even realize it, let alone understand it. "You don't have to say anything," I continued. "Your medallion will speak for you. All you have to do is go stand with those guys."

Here's the thing: O'Malley was a marine, and they weren't represented by a Congressional Medal of Honor winner on the stage. Not yet. "There are a lot of marines in this audience who would go nuts," I pointed out. "They need to see one of their heroes up on that stage."

This time O'Malley didn't answer. He just stood there. Then he said, "You know what, Jon? You're right. I'm going to go up on that stage."

He made his way to it, and the marines went crazy, absolutely freaking crazy. And get this: O'Malley didn't stop once he reached the stage. He made his way to the microphone and said a few words. I don't know what he said, and I don't know if I could even hear it the crowd was going that wild.

One of my most cherished possessions is a picture of those men on stage with Wolfman Jack.

Before I went back to where the Minnesota delegation had camped out, I got their signatures on my book of all the war dead. It was hard to even get back to my table there was so much crying and hugging along the way.

The room was one big champagne bottle of emotion that had been shaken before being uncorked tonight. Three thousand soldiers had kept more than a decade of tears at bay somehow. Now every last drop rained down on us. It felt like we were being baptized.

You looked in any direction and there were guys in wheelchairs with both legs gone. For fifteen years we'd been stranded on some God-forsaken island of misfit toys, and just when we'd given up all hope of being discovered, this. We were being scooped up, dusted off, and repaired. Our bodies might look the same as they did when we arrived in D.C., but we were not the same. We had left our deformed psyches in a rice paddy and now we were getting them back. Not in mint condition, mind you, but we were reclaiming them just the same.

The bedlam died down to what was truly still a roar. The music started up again and the beer flowed. I was exhausted and exhilarated at once. "When I get home," I told Clark, "I am going to give the Memorial Day speech in Fertile that I've been asked to do for so many years." If O'Malley could do what he did in front of thousands of people, I kept thinking, I could speak to a few friends and family members.

There was no cadence on the flight home to Minneapolis. I was wiped. The only thing I remember about the trip to Minnesota was asking the stewardess for a pillow.

Before we left the Twin Cities we met with the commissioner of veterans affairs for Minnesota. I asked him if anyone had a book on the Congressional Medal of Honor recipients. "Yeah," he said. "You can buy one for ten bucks." So I did. Clark, Roger, and I jumped in my Scout for the trip home. "Look up Gary Wetzel's name in that book," I suggested. I never did find out what had set Gary off, after all, and I was curious.

Clark found his name right away. He gasped.

"What is it?"

"When do you think Gary Wetzel earned the Congressional Medal of Honor?" Clark asked.

No way.

"The eighth of January, 1968," I said.

"Exactly," he told me.

I had lost two limbs that day, Gary one. He was the helicopter door gunner. When his chopper was pinned down by enemy fire, he kept firing despite being badly wounded. He then helped his fellow crew members to safety, passing out twice from loss of blood in the process.

What were the odds, I thought, of meeting someone wounded the same day I was, a Congressional Medal of Honor recipient at that? That was really something.

I would return to Washington, D.C., many times. Every time I took a cab to the Wall, and every time I stood before it I cried. I just bawled my eyes out.

You don't stop visiting the grave of someone you love just because you've been there once. The bodies of my friends are not buried at the Wall, but that's where I feel their presence. But there's something else. It's almost as if this is the one place it's truly okay to cry. It's easier to cry there. Almost everyone does, it seems, and no one thinks anything of it.

Every time I return to the Wall, I remember something else about the war. The healing will continue, I'm sure, for as long as I live.

The next spring, I got to work on my third vow: to make a difference with my life. I can't remember who I called, but I told them I was finally willing to give the speech on Memorial Day at the Fertile-Beltrami high school. Not only was I willing, I was compelled. I had to start speaking about the war—I had to. It wasn't about paying the town back, though I certainly felt that obligation. It was more about finding an outlet for feelings I could no longer contain.

The program was at ten o'clock in the morning, right after the parade. It was a beautiful spring day in Minnesota, perfect for my speaking debut.

I hadn't prepared anything, hadn't even made any notes. That wasn't my style. I may have been a chickenshit, but I was also stupid. I wasn't going to prepare for a speech, even one as important as this one.

Five hundred people came. That beat Memorial Day attendance in recent years by about four hundred. It wasn't a big-deal holiday anymore, which I thought was kind of sad, though I also realized I could help change that.

Five hundred people may not seem like very many, but it represented more than half the population of Fertile. The program was in the gym, and it was hard to fit everyone inside.

We'd put up a couple of TV sets, and the first thing I did was play the tape of *Night Times Magazine* from Gary Gilson. When the video got to the part where Clark was pushing me in a wheelchair down Constitution Avenue in the parade, everyone jumped to their feet and applauded. I don't know who was more moved, me or them.

I was swept up right along with the audience. It was as if I was watching the dedication of the Wall for the first time myself. At one point they showed part of the Vietnam Veterans Memorial Vigil, where people were reading aloud the names of every soldier who'd been killed. It was heartrending. A lot of parents and brothers and sisters had wanted to read the ten or fifteen names closest to their son or brother so they could be the one to read that name. Then they'd reach it and not be able to get it out. It just tore you up.

Gary interviewed a nurse after she left the chapel and she talked about guys she remembered. She didn't know any of their names and that bothered her. She didn't know if any of them were still alive.

I wondered if that's how Nurse Kay felt. Did she remember me? Did she ever think about me?

As the crowd took in the Gilson tape I congratulated myself for letting that do most of my talking. I did say a few words after it was over. I talked about the day I got wounded—and the three vows I made on the ice blankets.

The thing was, everyone already knew my story. They'd read about it in the papers, they'd heard about it at dinner when parents were bringing their young kids up-to-speed on Fertile's piece of America's history.

But they had never heard it from me. I don't know what it's like to get up in front of a group of people and say, "Hi, I'm so-and-so and I'm an alcoholic," my postwar coping strategy notwithstanding. But I can't imagine it being much different from what I was going through that day. I felt vulnerable up there, talking about what I'd been through and what I was still going through. In some ways I was more frightened that glorious spring morning than I'd been on the worst night of ambush patrol.

When it was over, one emotion swept over me: peace. I mean, granted, this was a safe place to test my newfound need to speak out. I could have probably talked about the stock market and wowed the crowd. They were my family, my friends. They laughed, they cried, it was the feel-good Memorial Day celebration to end all Memorial Day celebrations, at least in Fertile. But the thing that lingers from that day is peace.

Suddenly the war was okay to talk about. I had finally come to terms with Vietnam enough to discuss it in public. I was richly rewarded immediately. I felt embraced. The appreciation I felt from the audience fueled my desire to reach out to other veterans.

I was asked to speak a lot after that, and until Darlene started to worry about me, I never once said no. Most of the invitations came from schools and I happily obliged. I brought my slides from the war and showed them to the kids.

My life after Vietnam was divided into two parts, before the Wall and after. Before the Wall you couldn't get me to talk about the war. After the Wall you couldn't shut me up.

I hadn't been back in Fertile very long after retiring from 3M when I was asked to run for the school board. No thanks, I said. I was still trying to heal. It wasn't that it only paid twenty-five dollars a meeting. I just wasn't sure I wanted to be on the school board, that's all.

"There's a lot more to it than buying toilet paper and paper towels," I was assured.

"I wouldn't doubt that," I said.

The pressure didn't let up and eventually I gave in. I ran for the school board and served on it for the next sixteen years.

I didn't stop with the school board. I got very involved with our church, Concordia Lutheran, where I had been baptized and confirmed. I taught Sunday School and was president of the church council.

Then someone asked me to serve on the Polk County Fair Board. "Well, yeah," I thought. "That's important, too," so I became treasurer. We were the fifth-largest county fair in the state and started bringing in talent like Lorrie Morgan and Dan Seals. It was fun, but that didn't pay much either—I think we got like three hundred dollars a year. Well, that, and a bunch of photos with celebrities. One wall in my office was plastered with them.

Then I was asked to run for another school-related board, the Region One Board. The people on that take care of all the state records and paychecks for about fifty schools in the northwest part of Minnesota. Fertile hadn't had anyone on that board for a number of years and someone had said I'd make a good addition. So I thought, "Well, yeah, why not?"

Then I got on the Northwest Service Co-op Board, responsible for buying school supplies ordered through the state.

And I was vice chairman of the American Legion.

There was no Kiwanis, no Rotary, but plenty of everything else.

It wasn't like I replaced all the hours I put into 3M with service work, not at all. There was no real pressure, no real deadlines, and even with everything I got involved in, I still had a lot of free time. Also, the time I did spend working was mostly sitting in meetings, so it wasn't at all hard on my foot.

I had a lot of meetings at night, but they were fun. They kept my mind active and helped me feel productive.

Darlene wasn't concerned about any of it. It just wasn't the same grind as at 3M.

When I got into school board work, I really felt like I could make a difference in the lives of kids. I knew right away that was going to be more rewarding than a paycheck from some corporation, and it was.

Public education was taking such a beating in the press back then. It seemed like public schools were always on the front page of the newspaper for one reason or another. There were so many stories about test scores being so bad, things like that. And I kept thinking, Minnesota's test scores are among the highest in the nation—how bad can it be?

Arne Carlson was governor at the time. He had gone to a private high school and his undergraduate work was at a private college. I always got the feeling he didn't think much of the public school system, but maybe that was just me.

My feeling was, you don't build things up by tearing them down. You just don't.

I really got into school board work and eventually found myself on the state board. That's made up of fifteen different directors from across the state. The northwest district seat was opening up, but I don't remember how I actually got involved in running. Somebody just said, "Hey, you need to go on it and represent us." And I thought, "Well, yeah, I could do that I suppose."

A few years into my service with the state board, I was nominated to be president of the Minnesota School Boards Association. Twenty-two hundred members, and most of them, it seemed, were at the Minneapolis Convention Center for the annual meeting in January 1996. Paul Brinkman from the Iron Range nominated me. He was on the state board at the time, too. Nobody was running against me, so they could elect me right from the floor.

Paul and I sat together in the front row. He showed me how he planned to introduce me. Then he asked where my speech was.

"I don't have one, Paul," I admitted.

Paul looked back at the crowd and then at me. "Jon," he said, "there are a lot of people here. You can't just wing it."

"I have to," I countered. "I need to connect with this crowd, and I'm not going to do it by reading notes off some card. Public education is under fire right now, and if I'm the guy who's chosen to lead this group, I'll do it. But if I can't make an impression by being myself, what's the point?"

What was he going to say? It wasn't like I had time to write something up.

Now it was Darlene's turn.

"I want to read your speech," she said.

"I don't have one," I told her.

She was worried, too.

It didn't occur to me at the time that I had merely traded one ladder for another. I kept telling myself I didn't really want the job. I was about to give a speech to about two thousand people, and until then I'd mostly only spoken to relatively small groups of people at 3M, or twenty kids in a classroom.

I was nervous.

I walked up on stage, wearing my three-piece suit and a Fertile Falcons hat from our high school boys basketball team. I had two good luck charms with me, a letter from Chaplain Vessels and a letter from Chaplain Ostroot. This was the only time I'd carried them in my life and I had them in my breast pocket. As soon as I took that first step, I tapped those two letters on my chest and said to myself, "You guys just tell me what to say."

That's the honest-to-God truth.

I couldn't tell you what I said at first, I was that nervous. I was a little choppy for a while, I'm sure, but it wasn't long before a calm came over me, and I talked for eighteen minutes. I know this because Darlene timed me. She told me later she couldn't believe what was happening, that's how focused I was.

I talked about my three vows. I talked about being wounded. I talked about kids. I talked about my friend who was a carpenter, who always said if you're building a house and putting up the walls, but someone is on the back of it tearing down the walls, that house is never going to get built. I told them if it was so obvious, why was the same thing happening to public education? "You have people tearing down public education," I said, "and we're trying to build it up. We need to get everybody together on this. We need to build. We need to build on what we're doing right."

That was a defining moment for me. I noticed some people were crying as I talked, and when I finished there was nothing but thundering applause—and more tears. I couldn't believe it. I had touched them. So much so that the executive director, who'd been waiting for me offstage, hugged me and said, "Jon, please don't make me cry anymore."

I was still talking to him when Paul Brinkman came back to get me. "Jon," he said, "you have to go back out there. They're giving you a standing ovation and half of them are in tears."

I walked back on stage and saw for myself. I tipped my hat and looked out into the crowd. Everybody was still standing and Paul was right, many of them were crying. "My God," I thought, "something really special has just happened."

Another superintendent came up to me after I left the stage again and said, "Jon, I want to tell you something. I've been coming to these things for more than twenty-five years, and I've never seen an incoming president be received like that. You really inspired these school board members."

Another speaker that day—he was on the national circuit and got paid like three thousand dollars per gig—caught up with me later and said the same thing. "What strikes me," he said, "is that there's not an ounce of bitterness in your voice." He paused. "I've never met a Vietnam vet who wasn't bitter in some way."

I get that a lot. People can't believe I'm not bitter. But I'm not.

I was basking, I admit it. I felt like a battery up there on stage with two thousand cables hooked up to me, charging me up. Maybe that's what I was put on this earth to do. Maybe this is what it's all been leading up to. Because the feeling I got in front of that audience, connecting with what seemed like every single one of them—what a high. I'd never been one for drugs, but I was damn sure this feeling was better than any drug.

To think of those two letters from my chaplains tucked inside my pocket and giving me confidence, well, it just tied everything up in a nice bow. They had said one day I'd be touching thousands of people, and I could see that happening.

Darlene had been worried I wasn't going to have anything to say when I got up on that podium, and now she was worried I'd never stop talking. Because from that point forward I started being in demand as a speaker—and had my usual trouble turning anyone down.

This was the first time I had talked about Vietnam in great detail with a big audience. I loved speaking to kids, but I didn't know how I would do with a big audience . . . of grownups. Doctors and dentists and lawyers, you name it. And I *loved* it.

Even today when I get home after a big speech somewhere—like an AFLAC convention in Tyler, Texas—my head stays puffy for a while. And eventually it wears on Darlene. "Okay," she'll say. "You're home now."

This feeling built gradually, of course. After that first speech I was just excited about connecting with school board members because it was my job. All I wanted was to touch a nerve, because if I could get them fired up I thought we could do some good things for kids. That was my only objective at the time. It wasn't to launch a speaking career.

At the first meeting of the state association I attended as president, I held up my right hand and said, "You see this hand? There's no ring on this finger. There's nothing to kiss here. I don't need to be called Mr. President." That's what they did in meetings before I came along—they addressed people that way. I thought it was a bunch of crap. We weren't in the Oval Office, for Christ's sake. Until then they had been expected to wear suits and ties to the meetings. "I don't care if you come in blue jeans and sweatshirts," I told them, "as long as you show up ready to work."

One of my first assignments as state president of the MSBA was to appear in a video that would be used to train new school board members. Wendy Wustenberg worked with me on that during the spring of 1996. She was the media consultant for the MBSA and we became good friends. Wendy suggested I lift parts of my speech for this video. Talk about what's right with public education, she said.

It was about this time I found out that Chaplain Vessels had died. I'd tracked down his brother, who was a Catholic priest in Atlanta. He sent me a photo of Vessels that still hangs in my office and told me he'd died several years ago after a second bypass surgery. When I opened the envelope with his picture inside, the tears started coming. They wouldn't stop, either. That face! It was exactly as I'd remembered it. Darlene was out feeding the horses and when she got back to the house she wanted to know what was wrong. She looked at the picture I was staring at and knew that was him.

I couldn't stop looking at the photograph. It was as if no time at all had passed, and I was back in the hospital with him cheering me on. It got to me, that he was dead—because he was a big reason I wasn't.

"We need to go for a walk," I told Darlene. We hadn't even gotten to the end of our driveway when three geese flew so low we could practically count their tail feathers. They were a scattered flock. "If I had my goose call," I told Darlene, "I could call them in."

The next morning I was supposed to be on the capitol steps to shoot that video for the school boards association. Wendy wanted me to think about what I was going to say, so that was on my mind. Another goose flew over as we kept walking. It was almost like Vessels was talking to me. Ostroot, too, for that matter. "The school board members are a scattered flock, Jon. You have to call them in. Get them V'd up and on a mission."

It sounds a little corny, I know. But by the time we got back from our two-mile walk I knew exactly what I needed to do. I called Wendy and said, "You have to get me with some geese." Just the thing a media consultant loves to hear at the last minute, but she was good about it.

She took me to the College of St. Catherine and we taped a segment on this little steel bridge. There were geese all over the place. There was a two-man camera crew, with their big white screen. "How are we going to get everybody on this bridge?" I wondered. It was just a one-way walking bridge.

"Don't worry about it," Wendy said. "You won't even notice they're here."

She was right. We got set up just as a flock was coming in. "Call them," she said. I blew my goose call and a photographer captured the whole thing. It went flawlessly. I started talking. I explained how when geese are in a V formation you can't call them in. They're on a mission—they're going somewhere. The goose in front leads for a while, then backs off, and the next goose moves to the front of the V.

It's brutal in the front, taking the brunt of the wind. It's also a very efficient way to fly. Geese can fly 71 percent farther when they're in a V, from what I've read.

The more I learn about geese, the more I use them in speeches as a metaphor for my life. When a goose gets sick, he heads for the ground and two other geese go with him and stay with him until he gets well enough to return to the flock. No goose is left behind.

Geese mate for life. When I started to do a lot of speaking it was at the height of the Clinton-Lewinsky scandal. I remember some high school boys whistling when I showed one of my slides from Vietnam. "What the—?" I thought. I had no idea what they were whistling at. I looked up at the screen, and there was a picture of Darlene next to my hospital bed, looking fetching in her miniskirt and all. In fact that's one of her fondest memories of Letterman. There may have been a lot of wounded boys in there, but they were still boys, and she got quite the reception when she visited.

I laughed with the boys in the audience. "Yeah, she's good looking," I said. "Still is." And then something just came over me. Ordinarily I would never share something this personal in a speech—hard to believe, considering what I've revealed in this book—but I knew that with what the president of the United States had apparently been up to, it wouldn't hurt to offer a different kind of role model. "And I'll tell you something," I continued. "We've been married for thirty years and I have never cheated on her once. That's just not what you do." I left it at that. You don't want to lecture after all. But I was stunned by their reaction to this little tidbit. They applauded.

The state school board members were scattered across Minnesota and we weren't going to get anything accomplished unless we found a way to unite. We had to come with one voice to the politicians and say, this is the way it is. If you're scattered, they'll just pick you off.

Wendy asked me questions for, I'm guessing, ninety minutes

while we were taping. She said they'd edit everything before assembling the video. That night I woke up drenched in tears. My pillow was soaking wet. Wendy pumped my heart out about Vietnam. She dragged things out of me I'd never talked about with anyone else.

I didn't know what it was. Wendy and I had a connection, that much I knew. She wasn't even sure she was going to take this job until after my speech in January. "With this guy leading," she told another colleague of ours, "we're going to do some great things for education." That made me feel good.

The more she and I talked, the more I started thinking about a book. I was already writing down some of my stories so my kids would have them, and it seems like every time I gave a speech more people asked about a book.

It was going to take a lot out of me, though, no doubt.

I had such a positive reaction to the video I started using my goose call in speeches a lot. There was a speech in Brainerd to some superintendents and I wasn't supposed to be the main attraction. "Just get up there and say it's been nice working with all of them," the man in charge suggested. "Tell them the dinner was good. Tell them about the video. Then introduce the next guy." That didn't sit well with me. It was almost like he was saying, be boring. Don't tell them anything that might actually move them.

I'm not big on authority. The minute you tell me what to do my first reaction is to say fine. Then I go do whatever I want.

Wendy knows this. The person in charge was trying to get reassurance from her that I'd stick to his script, but she knew better than to give him any.

I looked at the guy who was going to be speaking after me. I glanced at his pages of notes. There were a lot of numbers on them. He saw me looking at the stack and said, "Where's your speech?"

"I don't have one," I admitted. "But I don't think you're going to want to read from that when I'm finished."

It was time for my supposed few words.

I started with my goose call. I was at a microphone that was as effective as it was tiny, and I scared the shit out of people. Wendy and some others wanted to crawl under their tables, but hey, I had everyone's attention. I gave an abbreviated version of my standard speech—the geese, my vows, all of it.

The superintendents loved it. I got another standing ovation.

The people who were responsible for lining up the meeting were not impressed. They were really cool to me at the reception. Don't worry about it, Wendy said. She chewed on it, though. We were both really taken aback by their attitude.

Eventually she decided, maybe it was difficult for them to hear about my service. They hadn't served, though I've long since forgotten why. She thought maybe they felt guilty.

I don't know if they felt guilty, but some people do. Because they admit it. They'll tell me about avoiding the draft by going to college or—back when this was still a way around it—getting married.

I can understand guilt. I feel guilty! Everything I've been through as a result of my war injuries and I feel guilty I wasn't hurt worse. I can't explain it, but it's the truth. My closest friends from Nam—one of them, my brother-in-law, Keith—feel guilty I was wounded and they weren't.

I feel guilty my friend Dick Godbout was killed and I wasn't.

CHAPTER 8

Once a Fighter

It broke Dick Godbout's heart to think he wouldn't make it home to his wife. It broke my heart when it turned out he was right. And I mean that literally.

I was in Washington, D.C., on school board business in January 1991. I was walking near the Senate building with the president of the Minnesota School Boards Association. It was a warm day for January, and after several blocks I felt a burning in my chest. I didn't say anything to the woman I was with, but she knew something was wrong. When we stopped at a corner she finally turned to me and said, "Jon, do you feel okay?" I told her I did.

I really didn't think anything about it because I'd been having heartburn for a while. I never left the house without a package of Rolaids or Tums in my pocket, usually both.

I wasn't concerned, even though my dad had had heart troubles. He had died on Christmas Day, 1974, at the age of 73, and I had a couple of uncles who had made it into their seventies, but all three—both uncles, and my dad—had died of heart disease. I thought I was too young to worry about it. I was only forty-three.

I thought heart trouble meant a sharp pain in your chest, as opposed to this lower-grade burning sensation. I thought if it was serious, you'd feel a lightning bolt of pain. I didn't realize that with some people, it can be as subtle as an ache in your shoulders.

Once I got home from D.C. the heartburn, or what I thought was heartburn, got worse. It came and went, but usually lasted only two or three minutes.

That changed on March 25, 1991. Darlene and I were going to go for a walk when I decided against it. I had this burning in my chest again. "Go ahead and go," I told her, thinking maybe I'd lie down. But the minute she left it got worse. The pain got more intense the longer she was gone until I started to panic that she wasn't home yet. Back then she was working part time at the school and she was going to go there after the walk. "I don't think you should," I told her when she finally showed up. "I think you'd better take me to the doctor." Pause. "It hurts so bad I think I'll let you drive." She knew I must have been hurting because I would never have let her drive otherwise.

We jumped in my pickup and headed for Crookston. The doctor put me in the hospital right away, not because of my heart, but because he thought I had ulcers. That would make sense, I told him, because I'd been chugging aspirin for what seemed like forever to stave off the worst of the foot pain and whatever else.

They got my family history and some tests started to come back. I did have an ulcer. What a relief. At least it's not my heart, I thought. The doctor wasn't sure. He still thought there was a chance I was having heart trouble, too. He also wanted to know if I took Rolaids or Tums on a regular basis. You could say that. Antacids were second only to aspirin in terms of line items on our grocery bill. They were my top two food groups.

"Do you know what?" he said. "Eighty percent of the time when a young guy drops dead of a heart attack we find a package of Rolaids or Tums in his pocket."

That was interesting.

The doctor called a cardiologist in Grand Forks, who told him to send me to the hospital there. "Whatever you do, don't send him home," he added.

Darlene drove me to Grand Forks the next day. I'd barely gotten settled into the hospital there when I felt my heart flutter. They'd just hooked me up to a monitor. "Are you okay?" Darlene asked me. I hadn't said anything, but she knew. "Something just happened," she said. I told her it felt like my heart had skipped a beat. A couple of my friends had come with us to the hospital, but they left the room at that point, when my daughter happened to walk in. "Dad," she said, "are you okay?" Yeah, I lied. "You look pretty pale," she said.

All of a sudden the cardiologist bounded into the room. "I don't know what's going on with you, Jon," he said, "but we have to get you out of here and into intensive care."

They kicked someone else out of intensive care to make room for me, it was that serious.

My cardiologist had already performed two angiograms that day and wanted to rest before he did one on me. "We're going to get you stabilized overnight," he said. "You'll be fine."

By now both my kids had arrived, and they stayed with Darlene and me in the intensive care ward while I got hooked up to more monitors. Toward evening the nurse suggested they wrap it up. She wanted me to get some rest. There were hugs and kisses all around before they left and the melancholy set in. Okay, I thought, what's one more health crisis? But this one could be the mother of them all, I knew. This could be the end of the line.

"You know," this nurse said, "the woman who's going to be on duty during the night is the best nurse on the floor. She knows her stuff better than anybody. You'll be fine."

I didn't answer.

"You're thinking about dying, aren't you?"

I nodded.

"I can tell you're worried," she said, her voice getting softer.

"When they have to kick someone else out of intensive care to get me in here," I pointed out, "I figure it's pretty serious."

"It is serious," she admitted. "But if there's even the slightest change in your condition overnight, your heart surgeon can be here in five minutes. Every vital sign is being monitored. We're not going to let anything happen to you." She explained how the angiogram would work, details I can dispense with here. Heart trouble is probably like childbirth in that the same drama is being played out all over the world at any given moment. But if you're the one on the table, it's a different story.

I was surprised by the reassurance that I wasn't going to die. I couldn't help thinking back to the 12th Evac. There had been no reassurance then. I was in such bad shape and running out of time. The doctors and nurses hoped for the best, but prepared me for the worst. Maybe they wanted me to be able to make my peace with God if I didn't make it. They don't necessarily have time to pick the best way of breaking the news, after all. They tell you everything straight out because the next minute there might be bombs lobbed at the hospital.

I didn't really worry about dying after what this nurse had said. I still thought I might die, but that's not what bothered me the most. What bothered me more were my tennis shoes: my brand-new tennis shoes, still in the box at home, never having been worn.

"Damn," I thought. "I'm going to die—and I never even got a chance to wear them once."

Only weeks before I'd been to a new podiatrist in Crookston, Dr. Dave Peterson. "I'll have you in regular shoes in thirty days," he said. Yeah right, I thought. I mean, there was just no way. I'd been walking around in space boots for so long I thought of them as just another cross I'd bear the rest of my life. But they bothered me a lot. The snappy three-piece suits I wore during my days at 3M looked ridiculous when paired with those god-awful ugly shoes.

I'll never forget trying on regular tennis shoes for the first time since I was a kid. They were so light! It was like walking on pillows. My wooden leg was still so heavy, but regular shoes made all the difference. They may as well have had flubber in them, that's how much spring was suddenly in my step. I really looked forward to my walks with Darlene now. But I hadn't had a chance to go on one with my new sneakers. I was crushed.

The doctor made the angiogram incision in the same place in my groin that they'd used to thread the main IV into me back in Vietnam. He blew dye into my veins and I got to watch the whole thing on the monitor. As soon as he pulled the needle out he told me they needed my wife and kids in here so he could talk to all of us about the results.

"Your left coronary descending artery is 95 percent plugged," he said, "and you have two others that are 70 percent plugged." The left coronary descending is the widowmaker, he continued. "Do you know what I'm saying?"

I thought I did.

"What do we do?" I asked, trying to keep my voice as even as I could—for the kids and Darlene, if not for me.

"We need to schedule a triple bypass," he said. "Immediately."

"Is there any other option?" I asked.

"Yes," he said. "Death."

"Well, okay," I said, trying to chuckle. "Triple bypass it is."

I had the four-hour surgery on the afternoon of Good Friday, March 29. I woke up forty-five minutes after it was over. Normally people don't wake up for hours. In fact the guy who had

had one just before me, who also happened to be from Fertile, didn't remember anything for three days. I woke up in a panic because there was a hose running through my throat. I felt like a stuffed pig.

The nurses had given Darlene and me an instructional video to watch the night before. "Shall we put it in now?" she had asked. "Nah," I said. "What's the point?" It was the same old, tell-me-to-do-something and I'll just ignore you. Now I wished I had watched the video. I didn't know I'd be waking up on a respirator. Maybe if I had realized that I wouldn't be fighting it, and feeling like I was choking to death. Trying to breathe with this hose in my throat, not realizing the machine was breathing for me, was unnerving.

The pain was hard to bear. I was no stranger to pain, but this seemed worse for some reason. Not only that, but the morphine wasn't helping much. I think I had so much in Vietnam that it had long since lost its power for me. The doctor eventually told me I had enough morphine in me to kill a horse. "I figured that," I offered. "That's why I've been trying to get someone to just knock me out."

So I endured the same nightmare that any other bypass patient endures and was given the same lectures. I was supposed to stop eating crap and start getting more exercise. I knew it was going to be difficult to give up my Land O'Lakes cheese, but the exercise I could handle. I had new sneakers.

I thought my biggest challenge would be giving up cigarettes. I had had my last cigarette the night before I checked into the hospital in Crookston, although I didn't know it at the time. Actually I'd been smoking when I first noticed some chest pain. I'd been shoveling snow off the deck in our backyard and smoking, at once. Yeah, I know—how stupid was that? It was a heavy, wet snow, too, which made it even worse.

I didn't consider myself a heavy smoker. I smoked maybe

three-quarters of a pack a day. After the bypass the heart surgeon and I had quite a chat. We went on for so long that the nurse started banging on the door, trying to remind him that he had more than just me to attend to.

"Have you started smoking again, Jon?" he asked.

No.

"Are you going to take it up again?" he wondered.

I didn't think so.

"Do you own a handgun?" he said.

Yeah, I told him. I had a .357 Magnum.

"Let me tell you something," he continued. "If you ever feel like having a smoke, why don't you just load up that .357 and hold it up to your head? Go ahead and blow your brains out. That's what you'd be doing with the cigarette. Your death will come about that quickly."

I never craved cigarettes after that. Never. I haven't smoked one. Don't plan to.

Now I help other people quit smoking. My podiatrist, Dave Peterson, quit smoking right on the spot after a lecture I gave him when he started having chest pains. He's been off them for five years.

I never craved cigarettes, but I continued to crave Land O'Lakes cheese. I swear to God that company had to lay off five or ten people when I quit eating it. I had much more of a withdrawal from cheese than from cigarettes and to this day Darlene can't buy it. If there were a two-pound brick in the fridge, I would just inhale it.

I'm not big on authority, but something told me my doctor was serious about not smoking. I believed him when he said I'd be committing suicide if I started in again. I knew guys who had had bypass surgery but kept smoking—and none of them survived another year.

I celebrated my homecoming by having Darlene take a picture of me with my daughter Jessica on the night of her prom. Oh yeah. She was beautiful. But would you look at me! Forget the prom dress. Those tennis shoes are pretty dazzling, don't you think?

I'm not out of the woods when it comes to heart troubles. My cholesterol is way below two hundred, but that's only because I'm on eighty milligrams of Zocor. I'm on cholesterol pills and blood pressure pills and a pill that's kind of like nitroglycerin, which I take three of in the morning and three at night. It helps keep my arteries open. I also take aspirin and get frequent checkups.

I don't drink much anymore. You can't be on this much medication and tolerate alcohol. I don't miss it. I'll still have the occasional glass of beer or wine, but that's so infrequent I don't even consider myself a social drinker.

Our family doctor, Bruce Ring, keeps a close eye on me. We're good friends. He thinks all the aspirin I was taking probably saved my life—though it probably also gave me an ulcer.

I don't like drugs, but I pop aspirin like M&M's. At the time I was taking twelve to fifteen Vanquish a day. I have bone pain, I have arthritis in my neck and back, and my foot hurts all the time. I still go to a podiatrist every few weeks so he can carve away at the bone spur. Add to that all the aches and pains that are God's gift to the aging, and you have a boring old man with nothing to talk about except his latest health problems.

I'm probably down to six aspirin a day, and I'm trying to taper down even more. I want to learn how to tolerate pain better.

I began to pay more attention to the amount of stress in my life. Darlene helped with that. One particularly busy November evening when my speaking engagements were picking up, she grabbed my American Express calendar, where I keep all my lists of things to do and places to be. I was on my way to the horse barn and she took off after me, calendar in hand. "Jon!" she hollered. I stopped. "Do you know how many days you're going to be in a hotel this month?"

Well, no. I figured five, maybe ten.

"I'll tell you," she said. "Nineteen."

Really.

"What are you doing?" she said, in a tone that matched her "Oh no, you're not going back to work at 3M" voice. "You're not in good enough health to be doing this," she said.

Maybe I was, maybe I wasn't. I didn't really slow down after this particular conversation. I loved speaking too much. I would have to find something in it for her, that's all.

One thing we've come to realize, Darlene and I, is that I will probably always have to be reined in a little bit, and I will probably always resist it. I learned my lesson when it comes to chest pain, though. I don't ignore it. I call the ambulance right away. For the first few false alarms after bypass surgery I let Darlene drive me to the hospital and finally my doctor scolded me about it. "How would you feel if you dropped dead in the car and your wife was driving?" He had a point. I mean, granted I'd be dead. Still, that wouldn't be a very nice thing to do to her.

Another thing I started doing more of after bypass surgery was looking for more friends from Vietnam. I'd begun writing stories down for my kids. I'd get to a certain point and think, okay, I wonder what happened to that person. And then I'd try to find out.

I think I became more aware that I wasn't going to live forever, and I had more than my share of loose ends to tie up. More and more I thought of the stories my dad used to share with me about growing up in Norway. Then one day he dropped dead of a heart attack and . . . no more stories. How I wished he had written them all down. That was becoming more important to me, saving my story somehow. But before I could, I had some gaps to fill in.

The first person I wanted to find was Gary Platizky. He was from Brooklyn, New York, and had borrowed my penny loafers the day or two before I was wounded. He'd had enough time in country by then to get a week or so off, and had wanted to spend it in Hawaii like Godbout had, along with so many others. He didn't have any civilian shoes to wear on this break so he borrowed mine. I'd brought one set of casual clothes to Vietnam, which included a pair of penny loafers.

I knew the president of the New York School Boards Association and he loved trying to track people down. "If he's in New York, Jon, I'll find him," he said.

Turns out he wasn't in New York anymore—he'd moved to Arizona. I found his phone number and made the call. I recognized his voice the minute I heard it. "Gary," I said, "where are my penny loafers?"

There was a silence on the other end. Then he said, "Who is this?" I told him who I was, but he didn't remember me. "You're kidding," I said. "I was with you in Vietnam."

More silence.

And then, "I don't want to talk about that, Jon." Pause. "I just don't." I was so stunned and embarrassed that for a moment it was me who was speechless. "It got real bad over there," he continued.

"I know it did, Gary," I said. "Did you get hurt, too?"

"Well, yeah," he said, "but I really don't want to talk about it."

I could tell he was serious. "Okay," I said. "I'm sorry, Gary. Take care. Goodbye."

Didn't I feel like shit. I hung up with a sick feeling in my stomach. This guy was having his day, and out of the blue I call up wanting to talk about the good ol' days in hell. What an idiot.

It would be years before I thought seriously about trying to track down anyone else.

But one day early in 1998 I learned about the *In Touch* program. It helped the families and friends of Vietnam veterans find people who knew their loved ones. Requests were filed under the name of the veteran listed on the Wall, so they could put them in touch with whoever else might contact them about the same person. They were immediately swamped with requests. The people who started it were very careful about what information they gave out. The first thing they did was check a database for any Department of Defense information for the name on the Wall. They verified that information before putting anybody in touch with anyone.

In Touch had a Web site at the time, and I thought that was great. It was sort of a computer version of what I was hoping for in Washington, D.C., when the Wall was dedicated. I remembered going from hotel to hotel, hoping someone from my outfit would have written their name on a board in the lobby so we could hook up. But we never did. Now there was a way to possibly hook up with anyone in the world who might have served with me.

All I had to do was post my name on the site.

As eager as I had been to find people in 1982, some things had changed. Another fifteen years had gone by. Thirty years since the war. Why not just let it be? I hadn't been able to shake the memory of my disastrous phone call to Gary Platizky. More than anything, Gary seemed to be telling me this: Back off, Jon. You want to go back to Vietnam, take a hike. Or rather, a flight. Just don't drag the rest of us along with you.

On the other hand, as one child put it, once someone tells you not to put a marble up your nose, it's hard to think of anything else. Why would there be an *In Touch* program if everyone felt the way Gary Platizky did? People who are adopted often can't rest until they track down their birth parents, I reasoned. How many veterans were walking around missing a piece of themselves? I certainly was. I doubted I would ever be able to heal completely from the war, but until I found Nurse Kay, for example, there wasn't even a chance. And what about Dick Godbout's family? Surely they ached for details about his last day on this earth. I wasn't the only one who could provide those, of course, but I was the one he confided in just before his death, and there was a good chance I could provide some comfort by sharing even that much with his family.

It boiled down to this. I knew my mom and dad, my sisters, and Darlene would have been hungry for anything about my last day had I been the one who had died. Would Dick Godbout have done this for me? Would he have posted his name on this site, knowing someone from my family might be able to track him down as a result—and pull up all kinds of awful memories in the name of healing?

You bet he would have.

I typed in my name and made a wish on the send button. Please, dear God, help me find Nurse Kay.

Kay Layman was the person I wanted to find the most, no doubt about it. I hadn't come close to finding her all these years, but then again I hadn't exactly made it a full-time job. If she was alive, I wanted to find her. If she wasn't, I didn't necessarily want to know. The voices in my head battled it out.

Once in a while I'd mention in a speech that I was looking for her. One night a student from the Lake Park–Audubon, Minnesota, High School called. I'd spoken there recently. He wanted my service number, the dates I served, things like that. "What on earth?" I thought. I wondered if I should even give him information like that. Turns out he and some friends wanted to go online and see if they could find Kay.

What do you think about that? I asked Darlene. We were really touched.

Those kids didn't have any luck finding Kay, but they reminded me yet again how badly I wanted to. It was about this time that Wendy Wustenberg, my media consultant friend from my years with the state school board, told me she'd sent a letter to the folks who produce the television program *Unsolved Mysteries*. We were in California visiting Darlene's folks and that's where Wendy reached us. Her husband thought she was crazy. "Don't call him in California to tell him that," he warned. "Those people get thousands of story ideas, and there's no way they're going to call him."

The day after we got back from California one of the producers called. They were interested. They were going to help me find Nurse Kay. At the time, I didn't even know her last name. One day I was at my mom's and mentioned that. "I bet I have it," she remarked.

You're kidding.

"No, I'm not," she said. "I saved every one of your letters from Vietnam. It seems to me Kay's name is on one of them." She pulled out this box and it all came back. There it was, quite the record of my time in the war. I couldn't be very specific in letters home, but even as vague as my reports were they still brought back a ton of memories.

Mom was right, too. At the bottom of one letter it said, "I'm writing this letter for Jon. Nurse Kay Layman. . . ."

Oh my God. That was going to help, knowing her last name.

The folks from *Unsolved Mysteries* told me that if Kay was alive, they'd find her. They made plans to tape an interview with me. One of their directors flew in and spent five hours at my house. By the time he finished he told me he'd love to shoot a movie about this. He told me they had a place set up in Burbank where they could reenact my APC blowing up, the whole works. He said something like that might cost upward of $500,000 to film, but said they were prepared to do it.

But just as suddenly, the plans were scrapped. The guy called to tell me it was off. I asked why, but I knew. Nurse Kay was dead. "That's it, isn't it?" I said. "You found out she's dead."

"Oh no, Jon," he said, and there was a lot of compassion in his voice. "That's just the nature of this business. One minute someone thinks your idea is great, and the next minute it's somebody else's idea that's great. Please don't take it personally. It's still a good story."

I didn't care about the story. This wasn't about being on television. This was about Kay.

I didn't believe what he'd said, either. I worried that Nurse Kay was dead.

I knew Chaplain Vessels was dead—I had found out when we were shooting that video for the state school board. By now I'd also learned that Chaplain Ostroot had died of cancer in the early 1980s. It had taken so much out of me to hear about them, and I sure as hell wasn't eager to search for more bad news.

Some of the news continued to reach me, however, and not all of it was bad. Ned Seachrist from my outfit was one of the first people I heard from after posting my name on the *In Touch* site. He was on a track near mine the day I was wounded and remembered the explosion. His big dream in life, he said, was to come to Fertile and go on a two-mile walk with me. He and his wife, Cindy, flew to Minneapolis on September 30, 1998, and arrived at our house later that day. We went on our walk the next morning. It was the first of October and it was thirty degrees. Perfect, Ned said, enjoying the smell of oak leaves and the crunch of gravel under our feet.

In a letter to Mrs. Maurice Godbout dated March 18, 1998, Corky Condon from *In Touch* passed along contact information for me and told her I had served with Dick in Vietnam. They told her I would be notified that they had located her.

When I got my copy of that letter, months later, I assumed she wanted to be contacted. The people from the program had no way of knowing who did and who didn't, though that didn't occur to me at the time.

I was traveling a lot then, too, and didn't want to miss her telephone call if that's what she was planning. I tracked down her number online and called. The woman who answered was older, so I figured it was her. I introduced myself, but it didn't help. She had no idea who I was. Finally I told her I was the guy who was with her son when he died.

There was a pause.

"I'm sorry," she said. "I can't talk about that."

Not again.

I felt like shit.

"Oh, that's okay," I said. "I just assumed when I got this letter that you wanted to be in touch with me."

"I really can't talk about it right now, Jon," she said again. "I'm sorry."

And that was it.

Geez, I thought, *again*. This poor woman and I spooked her. I felt so bad about it. On the one hand, I wasn't about to not call in case she did want to hear from me—that was the chance I had to take. Still, it killed me to think I'd upset her.

This time I only had to stew a couple of weeks before someone took pity on me. This time it was Robert Godbout. When I checked my e-mail on June 12, 1998, there was a message from him. My heart stopped for a moment because Robert Godbout looked a whole lot like Richard Godbout when you're just scanning e-mails. He introduced himself as Dick Godbout's brother. He lived in King Ferry, New York, he said, and was a counselor. Actually he counseled people with post-traumatic stress disorder, PTSD. Some of his work was within the prison system, but he was also a minister.

Bob said his mother, "Mrs. Maurice Godbout of Manchester, N.H.," had received a letter from Corky Condon from the *In Touch* program. He said that he'd been frustrated for more than thirty years trying to find out what had happened to his brother. They had been very close, he said. Robert and Richard had three younger sisters and they were all still alive, as were both parents, Rose and Maurice. Maurice was a World War II veteran, Robert wrote, and had taken Richard's death "exceedingly" hard.

Robert was as eager to talk to me as Rose had not been. He was insatiable when it came to information about Dick. He told me how bad he felt at not being able to protect his younger brother. Bob was in college during the war. He hadn't gone to college to avoid the war, but he felt guilty that his brother had been over there when he wasn't.

Bob wanted to know absolutely everything I remembered about Vietnam, not just about Dick's experience there. I was happy to oblige. I looked at it as the least I could do for a friend. Dick was my friend and now Bob was. That's all there was to it.

When I first put my name on the *In Touch* site, I knew I might be signing up for something like this. That's why it took me two or three hours to actually type in my name and hit the send button. I thought it would be taking on a lot of responsibility—and it was, because I don't do anything halfway. If Bob Godbout wanted to know absolutely everything I could remember about Vietnam, then by God I was going to tell him absolutely everything.

It got to a point, though, where there wasn't anything left to tell. I may have even e-mailed him something to that effect. I'm sorry, Bob, I probably said. There just isn't anything else I remember.

The e-mails eventually went down to once a week, and then once every two weeks, and now we only correspond a few times a year. He seemed to have settled into some kind of peace where Dick was concerned, and I was glad about that. One reason I was so empathetic where Bob was concerned was that I had the same hunger for anything about Nurse Kay.

My friendship with Ned Seachrist continued to grow. His son was in law school and was very interested in all of his dad's stories. Joel heard about my search for Nurse Kay back before I'd given up on finding her and wanted to help. I gave him all the information I had on her, which wasn't much. But damned if he didn't track her down. It took months, but he did it. On June 30, 1998, I got another e-mail. "I think I've found her," he wrote. She'd been awarded the Army Nurse Corps Medal in 1972, and he was pretty sure this was the right Kay Layman. Everything's matching up, he said, adding that he really thought she was the one.

"If you call her and talk to her," Ned added, "I want to know right away." Ned's family was out of town, but he gave me the number where he was going to be.

My heart was racing as I dialed the number Joel gave me. The area code didn't work. I couldn't figure out what I was doing wrong, so I called Ned. Turns out the area codes had changed and we got the right one in short order.

I called the number again. "Kay's not here," the woman who answered said. I later found out it was Kay's roommate, Eunice. "She's in Ohio visiting her sister."

It was the Fourth of July, 1998.

No one was home, so I left a message. I went over to the neighbor's house for a little holiday picnic. I was too distracted to enjoy it very much, but I welcomed the chance to get away from a phone that wasn't ringing.

I went home a couple of hours later and checked my voice mail right away. There was a message! "Hi Jon," a woman's voice said. "This is Kay Layman, your nurse from Vietnam."

It was 2:23 p.m. I actually wrote that down. It was a big moment in my life. I still have Kay's message on tape, which included an invitation to call her back. We're going to be in and out a lot over the next few days, she had said, but go ahead and call.

I called right away, of course, but she wasn't there.

Damn.

How the hell was I going to wait?

I gathered up so many scrapbooks, everything I had on Vietnam, and looked through every page to see if there was anything she might be interested in. I assembled a notebook full of stuff and shipped it off to her.

She called back the next day, July 5. I bawled my head off the minute I heard her voice. I think she was a little taken aback by that. It may have even scared her a little, now that I reflect on it. She didn't remember me at first, she said, but as I described my injuries and the 108-degree fever it started coming back. She remembered which bed I had been in, and many other things about those twenty-three days.

We talked from 2:45 to 4:30. We might have talked longer, but her sister hollered for her to come down to dinner.

We talked once or twice more over the next few weeks and eventually decided we should try to meet. I told her Darlene's folks lived in California and we were planning to drive out there in October anyway. Usually we flew, but not always. This was a good excuse not to.

As always, Wendy Wustenberg was offstage, stirring more things up. She'd called a friend of hers from the *St. Paul Pioneer Press*, Rick Shefchik, after he did a piece on heroes. Wendy told him he should talk to me. "Just call him," she said. She didn't say why.

So he did. "Do you have some kind of a story?" he asked. "How do you know Wendy?" And we were off. He wanted to know when I'd be in the Twin Cities next and said he'd like to do a story on me. I met with him a few different times over the next few months, and what was going to be a little feature in the Sunday paper turned into a five-part series.

The story would end with my reunion with Kay, which hadn't happened yet. Someone from the *Pioneer Press* called the *Albuquerque Journal* and asked if they'd send a photographer to the hotel where Kay and I planned to see each other for the first time.

It was the middle of the afternoon of October 22, 1998, when Darlene and I got to Albuquerque. I'd been crying the last couple of hours, which I thought was good. There wasn't anything left, I was sure, so I could be composed when I laid eyes on Kay.

But who was I kidding? I hadn't been the slightest bit composed about anything since the Wall. Before Vietnam I never cried much. Men don't cry. Lutherans don't cry. Lutheran men of Norwegian descent *never* cry.

Except for me. I cried all the time, at least when I talked about the war, and dared anyone to think less of me for it.

I've had many vets walk out of my speeches because they couldn't listen without losing it. Many of them apologized for it later. Hey, I tell them, I've been there. No need.

Darlene and I drove up to the Hampton Inn, got settled into our room, and called Kay. It was about four o'clock in the afternoon. "Jon," she said, "the people from the *Albuquerque Journal* have been interviewing me. They want to know if you and I can postpone our meeting until the photographer can be there."

My heart sunk.

"How long?" I asked.

"How about eight?" she asked.

That was fine. Now I had time to buy her some flowers. I wanted to get her four or five dozen yellow roses. Darlene thought that was overkill. She thought a dozen would be okay. We settled on two.

We got a bite to eat, then picked up the roses.

We went down to the lobby at precisely eight o'clock.

Right away I saw a guy with a camera standing next to a gray-haired woman. That has to be Kay Layman, I thought. Then the dam burst. It was almost a primal scream. I would have been embarrassed had I been the slightest bit aware of anything except her arms around me.

Eventually I recovered a bit and we sat down. The cameraman hung back a little, but took a ton of pictures as we talked. I wouldn't learn this until later, but Darlene and even the desk clerks were under Kay's spell from the moment she opened her mouth. She has such a calming presence, such an ethereal way about her, that the manager of the hotel hated to get back to work because she could have listened to Kay talk forever.

Kay was so interesting that even I shut up and listened. Anyone who knows me can tell you it has to be really something for me to keep quiet very long. I'm used to having the floor and I rarely yield it.

Kay had gotten out of the service in 1980 and had been employed by civilian hospitals after that. She was a hospice nurse now, and talked about that work.

Kay told us that to her knowledge, no one else had ever tried to track her down. But she said it was an unspoken, unwritten

dream of a Vietnam nurse to meet up on the mainland with someone they'd taken care of.

She said she could tell I had been disappointed when we first
spoke on the phone and she didn't remember me. She'd cared for
probably thousands of men, though, so how would she have? She
said that while she hadn't thought I would make it at first, by the
time I left the 12th Evac she knew I would. It didn't really surprise
her at all what I'd done with myself. She knew I'd be fine. I had the
will, she said.

We talked for at least a couple of hours, but the time went
fast—much too fast. I was glad there was more to look forward to.

The next morning the three of us went out for breakfast,
then went back to Kay's house so I could show her my slides and
photos. I'm something of a pack rat, especially when it comes to
the war, and I think I overwhelmed her a little. She was gracious
about it, though.

Eventually we had filled in as much of the last thirty years as
two relative strangers could, and it was time to leave. "Thank
you," I kept saying. "Thank you. *Thank you.*" I felt so lucky to be
alive to thank her. I wanted to make up for all the guys who would
have wanted to, but couldn't.

Darlene said she was struck by Kay's kindness. Didn't it
bother Darlene, Kay wondered, that I had been so consumed with
tracking her down? To a point, Darlene admitted. But she always
told herself that if not for Kay, there would be no Jon, and she
tried to leave it at that. That became easier once the two women
met, Dar says now. There's just something about her. You can't
help but love her.

Kay said our visit helped her to feel better about her time in
Vietnam. She knew she had made a difference. She really mattered
to someone.

Did she ever.

The following year I started hearing from Dick Godbout's sisters. Cecile e-mailed me first, then Lorraine. Bob had been sharing different things with them. I think he kind of doled it out as he thought they could handle it. I had told Bob I'd be happy to talk to either or both of them, but I wanted them to initiate any contact. He thought that was a good idea.

In the fall of 1999, after I'd been corresponding with Cecile and Lorraine for a while, Bob mentioned that his family really wanted to meet me.

I think I'd been waiting for him to say that since his first e-mail. I was still sitting at my computer reading this particular message when I thought, I have to get to Goffstown. I had to get there and I had to start lining it up. Now! I mean, it was that urgent.

How was I going to make that happen? Oh, that's right. Ready, fire, aim.

I called Goffstown City Hall, introduced myself, and asked who I should be in touch with if I wanted to speak at their Memorial Day program the next spring.

"May I ask why you would want to come here?" the woman said.

"Sure," I said. I told her about my friend Dick Godbout.

"Oh my God," she said. "I graduated with him. I was in the class of '66 with him. Every time we have a class reunion we have a moment of silence for Richard."

There it was. Richard again. That's the first thing Bob Godbout mentioned, how strange it was to hear Richard being called Dick. At home it was always Richard.

It didn't take long to find the person who could give me the okay on speaking at the Memorial Day celebration, though I was warned that the year before they'd only had five or six people.

"This isn't about bringing in a big crowd," I reassured whomever it was. "This is about honoring a friend of mine."

Again it made me sad that more people weren't attending Memorial Day services. It seemed a shame to have one day out of the year set aside to remember, and then not to use it to . . . remember. Especially when you had someone from your own town who was killed in war.

"People are just too busy for things like this," I was told.

"Maybe we can change that," I offered.

The next thing I had to do was get the newspaper involved. Richard used to deliver the Manchester paper, the *Union Leader*, in Goffstown—probably another reason we'd bonded since I used to deliver *The Forum of Fargo-Moorhead*.

The more I had learned about Dick from Bob, the more I realized how alike we were. Dick liked motorcycles. I liked motorcycles. No wonder we'd hit it off.

I wrote a piece about Dick for Bob, and the *Union Leader* said they were going to publish it before Memorial Day. Whoever I spoke with was pretty sure I'd draw a big crowd.

Next I decided I really needed to talk to the kids in Goffstown, so I went online again and looked up Goffstown High School. I e-mailed the principal and asked if the kids could come to my speech on Memorial Day. Well, sure, he said. I e-mailed him again later to ask if I could speak to at their school, too. He'd have to think about that one, he said. Would I please send him some references?

Sure I would. One of them was from the executive director of the state school board in New Hampshire, who I knew from my own school board service. The principal and I later had a good laugh about his request for references. No hard feelings, I reassured him. He was just doing his job, and I respected him for that.

Darlene and I looked forward to the trip all spring. That's one thing I love about Dar. I tell her what I need to do and she's there. There isn't a lot of arm twisting.

When Ned Seachrist found out I was going to Goffstown, he wanted to come. He'd met Bob several months before. He had been out east for something, and they had met for lunch.

So in May, Darlene and I drove to Ohio, where Ned and Cindy joined us for the rest of the trip. Goffstown is a suburb of Manchester, and we stayed at the Manchester Ramada Inn. We got in about four the afternoon of Saturday, May 27, 2000. I called the Godbout house right away. Cecile answered and said Bob had just arrived. He was just going to stay long enough to say hello before going up to Vermont to pick up Dick's widow. Somehow he had tracked her down. His family had lost touch with her—in fact the last time they'd been together was just after Dick's funeral.

I thought the Godbouts would want us to come over right away, but Cecile suggested that since family was still arriving, maybe we could come over at noon the next day. They had a picnic planned.

There wasn't anyone around when we drove up to the Godbout house, at least it didn't seem like it. But we knew it was the right house, and the right time, so we walked to the door. "You knock," I told Ned.

"I don't think so," he said. No sense being shy now, he warned. "You're the reason we're here, not me."

I started crying.

"Are you okay, Jonny?" Darlene wondered.

I was more than okay.

I was home.

I knocked, and Dick's mother, Rose, answered the door. More tears. I can't remember what I said to her at first, but I'm sure it was something along the lines of, you know, I am just so sorry.

That's what was strange. It was as if Dick had been killed yesterday, and we were there to deliver the news.

The next few minutes were a blur, just a tornado of tears and hugs and introductions. Dick's dad, Maurice. His brother, Bob. His sisters, Cecile and Lorraine. His widow, Linda. Spouses. Some kids. More than one nephew with Richard for a middle name.

"Come on in, come on in," someone said, and we settled into the living room to talk. For all the commotion of our arrival, it got quiet pretty fast and pretty soon it was mostly me talking—about Dick, about the war, about the day he died, everything. After a while we went outside to where the barbecue was. We joked around and told lighter stories. Then we went back into the house for a while to pour our hearts out again. It went on like that forever. Back outside to eat and be merry, back inside for more tears.

It was almost as if Dick was saying, "Now, Jon, tell them everything you know. They need to know." There wasn't much they hadn't already learned by e-mail, but it was different sharing it in person. I felt embraced. I couldn't imagine Dick's family embracing me more if I *was* Dick.

That's *it*, I thought. It was as if *I* were the lost son who'd returned home.

I had plenty of questions myself. I wanted to know what it was like when Dick's body arrived in the States. "Jon, we were standing on the tarmac at Manchester's airport on the eleventh of January, 1968," Bob said. "It was Richard's twentieth birthday—can you imagine? My parents watched their son brought home on his twentieth birthday, watched his wife become a widow at nineteen."

We went outside for more food.

And so it went, for hours.

We hung around until about three that afternoon and looked forward to my speech the next day.

At five-thirty in the morning, Ned called, wondering if I wanted to go to the cemetery to see Richard's grave. "Gee, I don't know," I said. "I might want to wait until after my speech. I don't know if I can handle it." But it was really nice out and I was awake. There wasn't a whole lot else to do. Sure, I said. I'd go.

Ned said a few words at the grave, then waited for me to say something—but I couldn't. It wasn't that I was crying. I just wanted to save any expression of grief for my speech.

The program was at ten o'clock, right after the parade. Everything was on schedule since the weather was perfect. I rode on a float with Ned and several other veterans from Goffstown. The parade ended right where we spoke, a little area right on Main Street. There's a big statue of a soldier and they have a bunch of bricks with the name of a deceased veteran on each one. I took a moment to look at Dick's.

I made my way to the front of the crowd. The population of Goffstown is about seventeen thousand, and at least a thousand of them were there—the biggest crowd they'd ever had for Memorial Day.

This was the first time in my life I felt a need to work from notes. I just didn't know if I would make it through the speech. It was so emotional to have Dick's family listening. We'd brought his mother a dozen roses, Ned and I. Cindy and Darlene presented them.

I looked out at the crowd. Rose was sitting in a lawn chair, with Maurice next to her. They were surrounded by Linda, Bob, Cecile, Lorraine, spouses, nephews, and everyone else we'd met the day before.

There were a few remarks by other people before it was time for my speech. Bob gave the invocation. Then it was my turn.

I don't usually get nervous before speaking, but this was different—I knew it would be. I needed a good luck charm. Dad wasn't alive, but I'd wanted him with me so I had brought his pocket watch on the trip. The thing was, when we'd picked up the roses for Dick's mom, I had dropped the watch on the floor of the flower shop and the crystal had popped off. The glass didn't break, so I knew I'd be able to fix it. I didn't have time to fix it right then, though, and that bothered me. I'd wrapped it in a towel and stuck it in the glove compartment. At least it made it to Goffstown.

This was not your standard Hovde speech. Oh sure, I told a few of my own stories, but mostly I was there to remember Dick, so I told more of his. Most of them I didn't even have until the day before. I talked about the sugar maple trees he'd planted as a young boy. "Pop! Pop!" he'd said. "Can I plant these two trees?" Well, sure, his dad had said. He planted one of them in front of the house and one in the backyard. Somehow the one in the front became known as Dad's tree, and the one in the back became Richard's tree.

When I was at the house, I noticed how much bigger Richard's tree was than his dad's. "I bet you take pretty good care of that tree," I'd teased Maurice.

"Well, yeah," he said. "I guess I do."

"I bet that one gets a little more water, a little more fertilizer. . . ."

"Yeah," he said. "We do kind of keep an eye on it."

"You go by the Godbout house sometime," I suggested to the crowd, "and take a look at those trees. You'll see the difference." I found out later that Maurice thought that was really something, that all these people were going to be driving by now, looking at his trees. He didn't mind. "Maybe I'll put a hat out there so they can toss money in it," he said.

There were a lot of Harley riders in town. It was the unofficial start of summer and happened to be a perfect day for cycling. I didn't realize at the time that Harleys and Triumphs—Dick had had a Triumph—were not at all the same thing among motorcycle enthusiasts. No matter.

Dick Godbout wanted to be a motorcycle mechanic when he got back from Vietnam, I told the crowd. He loved his Triumph. And he told his brother, Bob, that if he didn't make it home from the war he wanted to be buried as close to the road as he could, in that cemetery on the hillside. He wanted to hear the motorcycle pipes crack as they roared through the valley.

I looked out on the Harley riders in the crowd. They weren't difficult to spot in their red bandanas. A few of them were nodding. "The next time you go down that valley," I suggested, "crack the throttle one more time for Richard."

I don't remember much of what I said after that. I was starting to lose my grip, and I knew if I kept going it would be over. I'd break down so bad I would never recover, so I wrapped it up in a hurry.

I walked over to the family when I was finished and hugged them all, one by one. I was crying, they were crying, I don't remember seeing anyone who wasn't crying.

People lingered in the park for a long time. It seemed like no one wanted to leave. What a gift to have blessed this town with, people kept telling me.

It was difficult to hear anyone, though, above the roar of an endless salute of motorcycle engines.

We went back to the house for lunch, then took Bob up on his suggestion to have a graveside service. It was pretty spontaneous. Everybody said something, even Lorraine, who added that this was really the first time in her life she could talk about Dick. She had been only nine when he was killed.

I was spent, just totally spent, so much so that by the next morning I wanted to call and cancel my speech at the high school. "If there's ever a speech you have to give, Jonny," Darlene said, "it's this one."

I knew she was right. I just didn't know how I was going to do it.

I got through it somehow, but when it was over you could have mopped me off the floor. That was before Bob read a poem he had written for the occasion. I couldn't help but think of a few lines from another poem he had written:

He waves goodbye.
Green airplanes fly.
The weeks go by . . .

Body counts.
Raging mounts.
Crowds protesting . . .

Time is slowing.
Brother fighting.
Writing.
Wounded . . .

At home, hearts exploding.
All despairing.
Waiting for the coffin to arrive . . .

Long, long, long wait.
Funeral wake.
Maybe a mistake?
Maybe a mistake?

The Godbouts had wanted us to come over to the house after we finished at the high school. I tried to get out of that, too, as I was drained. We did stop at the house before we left for Minnesota, but when Rose asked us to please just stay a little longer—they'd ordered pizza—I told her as gently as I could that we really had to get going.

I was exhausted, and we had a long trip ahead of us.

So we started saying goodbye. "Do you have to go, Jonny?" Rose kept saying. She hugged me so tightly I didn't think she was going to let go.

"Well, yes, Rose," I said. "I do." Rose was a peach. It broke my heart to say no to her.

"Will you come back?" she asked.

Sure, I said. I'd be back.

"Will you come back in a couple of weeks?"

We all had a good laugh before we cried some more, hugged some more, and finally said goodbye for now.

To them it felt like they were losing a son all over again, I think, and for a while I wondered if I'd done the right thing after all.

That feeling passed quickly. I'd been told all weekend how much it meant to everyone that we'd made the trip. I knew before we left that this was the most meaningful thing I'd done since the war. Nothing else even came close. Not even the Wall.

I knew from the minute we'd arrived that this was the final piece of the puzzle—at least for me. The last chapter. My healing from Vietnam was complete.

CHAPTER 9

Making a Difference

Much of what my kids were brought up to believe about the world collapsed on September 11, 2001. Much of what my kids were brought up to believe about me collapsed two days before that.

It was just another normal Sunday in many ways. I'd cut down six trees and spent the afternoon stacking wood. I should have been feeling worse about the butt chewing I'd given my son that morning, but I felt too justified. My first grandchild, Preston Jon, was about two at the time and had been bitten by a two-year-old girl. My then–daughter-in-law had taken him to her girlfriend's house, and it was the friend's daughter who'd had at Preston.

Preston was deathly afraid of this little girl, or so I kept telling everyone, and I wanted to know why they'd been over there in the first place. I lit into Jeremy about it on this particular morning, something to the effect of what the hell was his wife thinking? Something to the effect that he wasn't a very good dad.

He didn't yell back. He just took it. But he left without finishing the coffee he'd stopped by for, like he did every Sunday morning.

"You know, Jonny," Darlene told me in the kitchen after I

had finished chopping wood, "you have to apologize to your son and daughter-in-law."

"I can't do that!" I snapped.

I keep my pills on top of the refrigerator and without even thinking I scooped them all up and put them in a brown paper bag. I grabbed my keys, jumped in my pickup, and took off.

Way off.

I decided to drive to the mountains. I would drive to Montana to see the mountains, and once I saw them, I'd keep going. I'd drive right on through to California and drive this pickup off a bridge and be done with it.

There was no way I was going to apologize to anyone. I would rather have committed suicide.

Now this was a little extreme, even for me. I've always found it difficult to say I'm sorry. Doesn't matter what it is. Doesn't matter how clearly I'm at fault for whatever it is. It's just not my nature. It takes too much out of me. But this was unusual, even for me.

It wasn't typical for Darlene and me either. We have disagreements, sure, but we work them out. They're probably not any prettier than the next couple's, but they get worked out. Neither of us takes off, though, not even for a little while. So Darlene was worried from the moment I left. She wasn't used to me being this cold. And from the look on my face, she didn't think I was coming back.

I didn't come back. I got to Devils Lake, North Dakota, at about nine-thirty that night. I was starving, so I had some dinner at Kentucky Fried Chicken. I always carry cash on me, so that wasn't a problem. When I finished dinner I thought, well, I should call Darlene. She's probably worried about me. Why that hadn't bothered me until now, I can't tell you.

I called home from a pay phone outside a K-Mart in Devils

Lake. Darlene answered. "Jonny!" she cried into the phone. "Where *are* you? I've been so worried!"

I told her where I was, and I told her the plan.

"Jonny," she said, crying her eyes out now. "You can't do this! You're my life. There isn't anything left without you . . . "

We talked for a good thirty, thirty-five minutes, and somehow she convinced me to come home. I don't know how she did it. I got in the pickup and drove all the way back to Fertile. I got home about one o'clock in the morning. Dar was waiting for me, but we didn't talk much. We just went to bed.

Just promise me you'll call the doctor in the morning, she insisted.

I promised.

The next morning I sat in my office, still so angry about everything. Something possessed me to look up post-traumatic stress disorder (PTSD) on the Internet. I hadn't been reading very long when I walked into the kitchen and told Darlene I wondered if I had it.

Then I called Claire in Doc Ring's office. Just hearing her voice made me feel better. Well, better and worse. I started bawling into the phone and Dar had to take over. Claire's known me more than twenty years and she sounded as concerned as I knew Darlene was.

Doc Ring was booked all day, but asked me to come in during his lunch hour, where I continued to cry and carry on. "I wonder if you have PTSD," he said, before I could bring it up. He was doing his best to make sense out of what I was telling him. "Do you really think you would have killed yourself?" he asked.

I didn't know, but we all wondered, if I was serious, why I took my heart pills along.

Ring referred me to a psychiatrist, but not until after he put me on fifty milligrams of Zoloft. After a week I'd go up to a hundred milligrams. It was only going to be for three months. He also put me on sleeping pills. I wasn't going to be on them forever either, he said, just for now.

I kept the appointment with the psychiatrist. Ordinarily I wouldn't have, but considering what I'd pulled I thought I'd better lay low for a while—you know, do what I was told. After a couple of sessions the shrink said she couldn't be sure I had PTSD after all, so that was the extent of my therapy. By then the meds were helping so much we agreed that people would just start keeping a closer eye on me, and they did.

In fact, the very next weekend Darlene was going down to the Cities to be with our daughter, Jessica, who was pregnant with our second grandchild, Olivia. Clark came up and spent the weekend with me. He was supposed to come help me over a rough time, but the more we talked the more we decided, hell, he had it worse. Clark hasn't been able to cry since Vietnam. He'd always had trouble sleeping, but then every Vietnam vet I know has trouble sleeping.

I've never slept much, but until this episode I never thought much about it. I didn't have night sweats—or so I told myself. But I always sleep without a shirt on and without any covers. Otherwise I wake up drenched in sweat. Okay, so I do have night sweats.

I know one thing that contributed to my breakdown—and I hate calling it that, but there's no sense denying it—was my chronic lack of sleep. Since that very first night on ambush patrol I haven't had what I consider a normal night's sleep. As of the ice blankets my chances for a good night—or day, for that matter— were pretty much over, in that I'm probably always going to be on high alert, vigilant. I don't sleep very well or for very long.

When I was at 3M I would put up sheetrock down in the basement until one o'clock in the morning, then get up at five-thirty and go to work. When the kids were babies it was me waking up if they so much as turned over in their cribs. I didn't get up with them—that still fell to Darlene—because I needed the few hours of sleep I actually got.

Most people are a little out of it when they first wake up. Not me. I go from a dead sleep to fully functioning in one second. I'm wide awake, ready for battle.

The next time you're in church, notice who sits in the aisle seats. I'll bet if there are any veterans in the congregation, they're planted firmly in those. You always want to be ready to make your escape.

I didn't stay on sleeping pills after this episode because they made me too groggy, but they helped me get over it. I took them for two weeks and caught up on what felt like a lifetime of sleep.

Zoloft didn't really help me sleep, but it calmed me down a little bit. It mellowed me out more than anything, and once in a while I relaxed enough to take a nap. I stayed on it, too, after the three months were up, because it was helping so much.

Darlene can tell you, the difference Zoloft made was subtle and dramatic at once. She says that until I left for the mountains that day, probably 96 percent of the time I coped just fine. But that 4 percent was the rub. I'd lose my temper. I'd get stuck on something and not be able to let it go. Nothing abusive, nothing too strange. It would just be . . . tense.

Looking back, she wonders if at some level she didn't see the breakdown coming. I wasn't as happy-go-lucky as I used to be. I was more crabby. Things seemed to be building up.

It's ironic that I left Goffstown thinking, well, now I'm healed. Just when I thought all the loose ends had been tied up, everything began to unravel. It makes sense now. I'd been doing so much talking about Vietnam it felt like I was still there in some ways. Like life was a battle to be fought.

I'd only been on Zoloft one day when the World Trade Center towers were hit. I was as glued to the television as anyone else those first few days, all the while thinking, oh man, I didn't get on this stuff any too soon. Ask any veteran how it feels to watch coverage of what's going on in Iraq. You can say, well, just don't watch it, and sometimes I try not to. But there's a pull. It's almost like you have to watch. You can't tear yourself away. And then you pay for it with more anxiety.

I've seen World War II vets who are eighty years old and just coming down with PTSD. It's sad, to think of all they've been through for more than half a century that they're just now coming to terms with.

I used to be suspicious of some Vietnam veterans who claimed to have PTSD. I'd think to myself, crap, they never even saw combat. They just want their couple thousand extra bucks a month. If you come down with PTSD and can't work anymore you can go on 100 percent disability from the government. I didn't stand to collect anything extra because I was already on total disability.

I don't know if I had PTSD, or rather, if I *have* it. But I'll tell you what. I needed a brush with it to take me down a notch.

After the Wall, and especially after Goffstown, I was no longer Humpty Dumpty, or so I thought. I'd put myself back together just fine, thank you very much, and now it was time to help others.

What a crock.

The funny thing was, I seemed better able to help in this condition. The more I could admit I didn't have all the answers, or maybe any of the answers, the more veterans seemed to open up to me. Someone would e-mail me after a speech to say their dad hadn't been able to talk about the war until then. It was almost like a baton had been passed. I had convinced Bob O'Malley to get up on stage and help heal his friends. Now it was me on the stage, across Minnesota and the rest of the country, helping heal new friends I made almost every day.

I love public speaking. I want to touch people, and my speeches are a great way to do that. It's my way of making a difference. It's funny—at my age, fifty-seven, a lot of people are looking ahead to retirement. I'm trying to figure out how to get back *into* the workforce.

A question I get asked a lot now that I'm in the public eye is, "Do you have any regrets?" Children often wonder if I had it to do over again, would I have skipped to Canada? And I tell them, no way. "Absolutely not. Things happen for a reason, and I wouldn't change a single one of them."

You would think my most prized possession would be my Purple Heart. It's not. My most prized possession is a scrapbook of letters from kids who have heard me speak. One girl wrote to say that she was contemplating suicide and now she's not. It still gives me chills, thinking of that letter. Chaplain Vessels and Chaplain Ostroot kept me alive as I battled the ice blankets. They saw a life worth saving. I look at kids, and remind them how much they matter, too.

That's what a lot of kids are missing these days, it seems— reassurance that they matter. Some of them think life is only worth living if you're a star on the football team, or dating someone on it. They listen to me talk about what I've been through and the mistakes I've made, and they realize they don't have to be perfect. Life is still worth living. They're fine, just the way they are. They seem hungry to hear that.

I joke that it's not just kids who need to hear what I have to say. Their teachers need to see them in a different way. I can't tell you the number of times I've gone into a school, whether to talk to second graders or high school seniors, and almost without fail someone will pull me aside and say, "Good *luck*. This is a tough crowd." I've never once had a problem, though I suppose my hook is a pretty good reason to sit still while I talk. But it's more than that.

Kids are genuinely fascinated by what I've been through. "What was it like to be shot at?" they wonder. "Did you ever shoot back?" They want to know what it's like to live the way I do now. "Do you sleep with your hook?" they'll ask. "Can you swim? Can you clap?"

Sometimes I'll even pull up my pant leg and do a little lap around their classroom with my $42,000 titanium leg. You should hear the "oohs" and "aahs," especially from the youngest children, as I make my way to the front of the room again. I sit back down and explain that the leg has a hydraulic system that controls the knee, complete with computer chips and everything. "See these red dots?" I'll say. "I plug my leg into an electrical outlet and charge it up overnight."

It's fun what happens next. "I used to have to take my leg off to change my shoe or my socks," I say. "But this new leg has a button that lets me flip it up like this." I rotate the leg a 180 degrees so the bottom half is sticking straight up in the air, at a right angle to my upper leg. The children gasp.

I definitely have the wow factor going for me in schools. But I don't spend the whole time showing off. I talk about getting wounded, I talk about going through life without an arm and a leg, but I also talk about what life is all about. It's about helping your friends. In war they call it not leaving guys behind. In school that means not leaving someone out just because they're different. And if it's you feeling left out, you hang in there. Each of you was put on this earth for a special reason, I tell them, and it's up to you to discover what that is.

You've probably heard that you don't really have something until you give it away. That's why it meant so much to me in the spring of 2004 to present Kay Layman with my Purple Heart after I introduced her to kids at a high school in Moorhead, Minnesota. I hadn't seen her since our reunion in 1998, and to be able to tell a gym full of kids what she meant to me—with her sitting in the audience—will always be one of my life's biggest thrills.

I am a stronger person for having lost almost half my body. I learned to use my brain, for one thing. But it's so much more than that. I appreciate things I would never have even noticed had I not been to Vietnam. I am so impossibly thankful for the greatest gift, just waking up in the morning. Since the moment I got off the ice blankets I have never taken a single breath for granted.

What I love about my story is that I don't know what's going to happen next. Just as we were finishing the interviews for this book, I decided to go off Zoloft, pretty much cold turkey. I cut my dose by half on this whim, and cut it out altogether a week later. Not very gradual and no doctor supervision. Ready, fire, aim. It might be good, I decided, to write three different endings for the book.

Which is as it should be. I don't know how my story will turn out. That's why I'm always so eager to share the latest installment. There's apparently no such thing as a complete recovery from Vietnam. You can get better, and life—a good life—can go on. But you will never forget.

And why would I want to? Why would I want to forget Nurse Kay coming at me with the straightedge? Or Clark taking a .50 caliber to that bird? Or the monkey our outfit adopted as a pet, that went everywhere we did—until it learned to pull the pin on hand grenades? I look back on months filled with horror, and see so many smiles.

Most of all, I don't want to forget my friends. I want to ride off into the sunset, cracking the pipes on my motorcycle one more time, for Richard.

Jon Hovde is a veteran of the Vietnam War and was awarded a Purple Heart after losing an arm and a leg in combat in 1968. After the war, he returned to Minnesota, where he eventually became an executive in the 3M corporation and president of the Minnesota School Boards Association. He is also a motivational speaker and frequent guest on radio and television programs. He has been featured as the subject of a five-part series in the *St. Paul Pioneer Press*, as well as in many other publications. He is an Outstanding Alumnus of Minnesota State University–Moorhead.

Maureen Anderson is host of the syndicated radio program *The Career Clinic*®. She is coauthor, with Dick Beardsley, of *Staying the Course: A Runner's Toughest Race* (Minnesota, 2002).